A Guide to Non-Sexist Children's Books

Compiled by
Judith Adell and Hilary Dole Klein
Edited by
Waltraud Schacher
Introduction by
Alan Alda

ACADEMY
PRESS
LIMITED

First Printing, January, 1976.
Second Printing, April, 1976.

Library of Congress Cataloging in Publication Data:

Adell, Judith.
   A guide to non-sexist children's books.
   Includes indexes.
   1. Children's literature — Bibliography.   I. Dole,
Hilary, 1945 —   joint author. II. Title.
Z1037.A1A1016   [PN1009.A1]   028.52   75-34396
ISBN 0-915864-02-9

From *This Is My Father and Me* by Dorka Raynor

Acknowledgments

A great many people have been helpful to us in the compilation of this book. A number of feminist groups and publishers have readily provided information and review copies. We should especially like to thank J. Philip O'Hara and members of his staff; Pat Ross and Wendy Wolf of Alfred A. Knopf & Co.; and Bruce Miller.

We should also like to thank the following for reprint permission:

Dorka Raynor's frontispiece originally appeared in her own book, *This Is My Father and Me,* published by Albert Whitman & Co.

Two illustrations from Ilon Wikland's *I Can Help Too!,* published by Random House.

One illustration from *Mary Jo's Grandmother* by Janice May Udry, illustrated by Eleanor Mill, published by Albert Whitman & Co.

Two illustrations from Stan and Jan Berenstain's *He Bear She Bear,* published by Random House.

One illustration from *Nine Lives of Moses* by Marion Fuller Archer, illustrated by George Armstrong, published by Albert Whitman.

One illustration from *Rally to the Death* by Douglas Rutherford, cover illustration by Christopher Tipping, published by Bradbury Press.

Two photographs from the files of United Press International.

One photograph from the files of the United Nations.

Contents

PREFACE

The titles in this book have been divided into three broad categories:

  I Pre-School through Third Grade
  II Third Grade through Seventh Grade
  III Seventh Grade through Twelfth Grade

We have added a fourth category under which are listed titles suitable for "All Ages." Each of the three main sections has two subdivisions: Fiction and Non-Fiction.

  These broad categories are not meant to define rigidly the age or grade for which the book is intended. There is a good deal of variety in the appeal of these books. Some second grade children may enjoy reading books which have been placed in the Third to Seventh Grade category, for instance. On the other hand, quite often an eighth grade child may enjoy a book which has been listed for an earlier grade. There is nothing at all wrong with this: it is simply a matter of the child's taste or state of development. It should therefore be emphasized that *these categories are in no way prescriptive*, but merely *loosely descriptive* for purposes of convenience. One should also bear in mind that one can read a book *to* a child who can understand it perfectly and enjoy it, although he or she may not be able to read it himself or herself without some strain. This applies, of course, to all children, and particularly those with reading or learning disabilities. The child's taste should be the guide: it is important, however, that children be offered books at whatever level they prefer; in this way, children develop the *habit* of reading for enjoyment, a habit which offers lifelong rewards.

  In the annotation or description of each title we have included the name of the publisher, the date of original publication, the grade category into which the books *seems* to fall and the price of the book. If no price is given, this means that the book was out of print at the time this *Guide* went to press. Out of print books, of course, often can be borrowed from libraries or purchased second-hand: this is why we have included them. The publisher we list is the publisher of the hardcover book, although we have often included paperback prices as well. In some instances, however, the publisher of the hardcover and paperback edition listed is not the same. Books often move quickly both into and out of paperback print, so your bookseller might be asked to check *Books in Print* and *Paperbound Books in Print* so that you get an idea of the selection open to you.

Occasionally, we have noted that library copies (L) are available. This means that the publisher has printed the book to sell to libraries. The difference between a library copy and an ordinary trade edition is generally that library copies come without a dust jacket and with an especially sturdy hard cover. If the book is listed as being available *only* in a library edition, you should be aware that many publishers are quite willing to sell these copies to consumers through book stores. The price given in this *Guide* for a library copy may well be raised if one buys the book through a bookseller. The prices listed here in general are, of course, the prices at the time of printing this *Guide*; inflation may well change these prices at any time in the future.

We hope you will let us know what you think of this *Guide*. Since we intend to update and reissue it periodically, we need your responses to the present lists as we both add to and revise the book.

Judith Adell
Hilary Dole Klein
Waltraud Schacher

Academy Press Limited
176 W. Adams St./Chicago IL 60603

AGE-GRADE CHART

Age	Grade
0 - 4	Pre-School
5	Kindergarten
6	1
7	2
8	3
9	4
10	5
11	6
12	7
13	8
14	9
15	10
16	11
17	12

ABBREVIATIONS

Gr.	—	grade
PS	—	pre-school
K	—	kindergarten
+	—	and up
P	—	paperback
H	—	hardcover
L	—	library copy
n.d.	—	no date

INTRODUCTION

Stories for children are like dreams that we share with our kids. And since dreams can be rehearsals for reality, it's important what roles they find to play in those stories.

As a child I enjoyed seeing myself as the little boy in those books who always came up with the solution to the problem, protected the girl, and found a way to turn his old apple crate into a soda fountain. On the other hand, gradually I came to learn that I had to find the solution all by myself since the girls in these stories were useful mainly for standing around waiting to be protected. (We didn't know how *able* girls really were since we weren't encouraged to mix with many of the real kind.) It got to be something of a burden.

There was always a tremendous emphasis on winning, succeeding and being first. I remember a book when I was eight years old about the "Top Horse at Crescent Ranch" and the boy who kept him Number One. After I read it, I wrote a story about a horse who was *not* the top horse at Crescent Ranch. Even at that age I was becoming interested in horses who were only human.

To be sure, there's some pleasure to be had in winning, but not when half of us are considered to be incapable of winning and the other half incapable of ever losing. The stories listed in this book are the kind that treat boys and girls as people who have the same kinds of frailties and strengths. I think one of the great advantages of a children's literature like this is that some day soon men and women will think of each other less as strangers or aliens from another planet and more like the brothers and sisters we really are.

Alan Alda

Chapter One

Pre-School through Third Grade

From *I Can Help Too!* by Ilon Wikland

PRE-SCHOOL THROUGH THIRD GRADE

FICTION

Adoff, Arnold
BLACK IS BROWN IS TAN   Gr.K-3/$4.95H

Harper & Row, 1973

> The story of an interracial family done in rhyme.

Alexander, Martha
THE STORY GRANDMOTHER TOLD   Gr.K-3

The Dial Press, 1969

> When her grandmother asks a black girl what story she would like to hear, the young girl replies by telling the story herself in patomime.

Anderson, C.W.
A PONY FOR LINDA   Gr.K-3,$4.95H

Macmillan, 1951

> The odd coincidence of two inveterate horse lovers named Linda who meet at a horse show, win top prizes and end up becoming the very best of friends.

Ardizzone, Edward
DIANA AND HER RHINOCEROS   Gr.K-3

Walck, 1964

An ailing rhinoceros has escaped from the zoo,
but capable Diana nurses it back to health.
When a group of armed men comes to take the
animal back, Diana turns them away.

Asbjornsen, P.C.
THE SQUIRE'S BRIDE   Gr.K-5/$5.95H

Atheneum, 1975

Originally a Norwegian folk tale, this is the
story of a rich squire who decides to marry his
neighbor's daughter. The only problem is that
the daughter has already decided he will not.
How she outwits the old man, despite his
collusion with her father, makes an amusing
tale.

Ayer, Jacqueline
NU DANG AND HIS KITE   Gr.1-4/$1.25P/$6.95H

Voyager, 1959

Some colorful glimpses of a Thai village as the
young hero, Nu Dang, tries to find his lost kite.

Babbitt, Natalie
PHOEBE'S REVOLT   Gr.1-4/$3.95H

Farrar, Straus & Giroux, 1968

The heroine's rebellion is a consequence of her
irritation with the fussiness and frills of her

Victorian clothing. She likes the simple and straightforward look of her father's garments.

Baldwin, Anne Norris
SUNFLOWERS FOR TINA   Gr.K-3/$.95P/$5.62L

Four Winds, 1970

A young black girl will not be deterred from cultivating her own garden even though she lives in the center of America's biggest city.

Behrens, June
SOO LING FINDS A WAY   Gr.K-3/$5.78H

Golden Gate Junior Books, 1965

Soo Ling helps her grandfather when his hand laundry is confronted with modern competition: an automatic laundry. How she helps him cope makes an engaging story.

Bemelmans, Ludwig
MADELEINE   Gr.K-3/$4.95H

Viking, 1939

Bemelmans' unique drawings accompany the story, told in verse, of Madeleine's appendix operation and the ensuing complications which involve others.

MADELEINE'S RESCUE   Gr.K-3/$1.50P

Viking, 1973

> The love of a dog proves stronger than the strictures of a boarding school in France. Madeleine and her friends set tradition on its ear.

Berenstain, Stan and Jan
HE BEAR, SHE BEAR   Gr.PS+/$2.95H

Random House, 1974

> A pleasantly-illustrated book in rhyme for new readers about what boys and girls can do when they become men and women. Men and women are depicted doing all kinds of jobs "whether we are he or she."

Blos, Joan and Miles, Betty
JUST THINK!   Gr.PS-3/$4.50H

Knopf, 1971

> Among other such happy phenomena are children in solid rapport with their fathers, a full-fledged, well-functioning day care center and a myriad of working mothers.

Blue, Rose
I AM HERE/YO ESTOY AQUI   Gr.K-3/$4.33L

Franklin Watts, 1971

> The difficult problem of a Puerto Rican girl adjusting to kindergarten is dealt with sympathetically, if somewhat superficially.

Boccaccio, Shirley
PENELOPE AND THE MUSSELS Gr.K-3/$2.95P

The Joyful World Press, 1971

Penelope is a venturesome five-year-old who flies a plane and takes care of her little brother. She takes him, along with a pair of attractive animal companions, on a mussel hunt.

Boegehold, Betty
PIPPA MOUSE Gr.K-3/$2.95P

Knopf, 1973

The various adventures of Pippa Mouse, whose activities include building a door for her mouse house, testing out a bird nest for sleeping and sliding on the ice on a birchbark sled.

Bonsall, Crosby
THE CASE OF THE SCAIRDEY CATS Gr.1-3/$2.95H

Harper & Row, 1971

A switch on the traditional order of things: the boys are the scairdey cats instead of the girls, and they lock the boys out of their own clubhouse.

Brownstone, Cecily
ALL KINDS OF MOTHERS Gr.PS-1/$2.95H

McKay, 1969

The bond of love holds both white and black families together whether mothers work or stay at home.

Burton, Virginia Lee
KATY AND THE BIG SNOW   Gr.K-3/$.95P/$5.95H

Houghton Mifflin, 1943

> No one could handle the snow which buried the city better than Katy the tractor.

THE LITTLE HOUSE   Gr.K-3/$6.95H

Houghton Mifflin, 1942

> The all-too-modern story of a little house in the pastoral, spacious countryside which loses its individuality as it is overwhelmed by the encroaching city.

MAYBELLE THE CABLE CAR   Gr.K-3/$4.23L

Houghton Mifflin, 1952

> The threat of "progress" is personified by Big Bill, one of the gasoline buses meant to replace Maybelle and the other San Francisco cable cars. But Big Bill is defeated by the San Francisco hills, and so the cable cars survive.

Byars, Betsy
GO AND HUSH THE BABY   Gr.K-3/$.75P

Viking Press, 1971

> Will keeps his little brother diverted through songs, stories, and sleight of hand.

Caines, Jeanette
ABBY   Gr.PS-3/$3.95H

Harper & Row, 1973

> A number of stereotypes are dealt with here:
> mother not only does household chores, but
> she is also seen studying. Abby, an adopted
> black child, successfully deals with brother
> Kevin whose boast that he does not like girls
> turns out to be false.

Caldecott, Randolph
THE MILKMAID   Gr.K-3/$2.95H

Warne, 1882

> How a young man looks for a wealthy wife and
> finds, instead, a young woman who knows her
> own mind.

Chalon, Jon
THE VOYAGE OF THE FLOATING   Gr.PS-3/$5.00H
BEDSTEAD

Bobbs-Merrill, 1973

> The fantasy adventures of a little girl.

Chapman, Kim Westsmith
THE MAGIC HAT   Gr.K-4/$2.00L

Lollipop Power, 1973

> The story of how toys came to be known as
> "boy toys" and "girl toys."

Charmatz, Bill
THE LITTLE DUSTER   Gr.K-2/$5.95H

Macmillan, 1967

A good-natured tale about a man who straightens up his apartment with the unwitting help of his dog.

Clifton, Lucille
DON'T YOU REMEMBER?   Gr.PS-2/$5.50H

Dutton & Co., 1973

Tate is a four-year-old black girl with a prodigious memory who is unprepared for the surprise her family has in store for her.

Cohen, Miriam
WILL I HAVE A   Gr.K-1/$1.25P/$4.95H
FRIEND

Collier, 1967

A little boy deals with the uncertainties of his first days in nursery school.

Cole, Joanna
PLANTS IN WINTER   Gr.PS-3/$1.25P/$4.50H

Crowell, 1973

The strange and interesting story of how plants are able to protect themselves in winter is told by a botanist to her friend.

Danish, Barbara
THE DRAGON   Gr.PS-3/$1.50P
AND THE DOCTOR

Feminist Press, 1971

A sick dragon is brought back to health by a young girl.

DeAngeli, Marguerite
THEE, HANNAH!   Gr.2-5/$5.95H

Doubleday, 1940

The story of Hannah and the Underground Railway which functioned before the Civil War. She comes to appreciate the significance of her simple Quaker dress as she helps to smuggle a black family out of the South.

Delton, Judy
RABBIT FINDS A WAY   Gr.PS+/$4.95H

Crown, 1975

One Saturday morning Rabbit is going to Bear's house to sample the carrot cake Bear always bakes on Saturday. But he arrives to find that Bear has overslept and couldn't make the cake. Rabbit, who had turned down several offers of food on his way, solves the problem by baking a carrot cake himself.

de Poix, Carol
JO, FLO AND YOLANDA   Gr.PS-2/$1.75L

Lollipop Power, 1973

> The similarities and differences amongst the La Raza triplets are shown. We also see the three girls with their friends and family and get an insight into their thoughts and dreams.

Eastman, Philip D. and McKie, Roy
SNOW   Gr.1/$2.95H

Random House, 1962

> An engaging story of two little girls playing in the snow.

Eichler, Margrit
MARTIN'S FATHER   Gr.PS-1/$1.75P

Lollipop Power, 1971

> One of the more instructive, sympathetic stories about the single-parent-child relationship. In this case, a father and his son cope with all the day-to-day problems of running a household. The story also shows the father and son in their lighter moments.

Ets, Marie Hall
PLAY WITH ME   Gr.PS-1/$3.50H

Viking, 1975

> The forest is presented as a friendly place, not a foreboding one, where a little girl plays by a pond and meets nice animals.

Fassler, Joan
HOWIE HELPS HIMSELF   Gr.1-3/$4.25H

Albert Whitman, 1975

>   A story about a handicapped child who learns
>   that even though he is dependent upon others
>   to perform some basic everyday tasks, he is still
>   an individual person. How he deals with
>   himself, his family, and his schoolmates makes
>   an instructive manual as well as a moving story.

Freeman, Don
DANDELION   Gr.K-3/$4.95H

Viking, 1964

>   A lion is "done up" in such an outrageous
>   fashion that he is not even recognized by his
>   friends. Luckily, he gets caught in a cloudburst
>   which washes out his curls and frills and he
>   resumes his normal appearance; as his real self
>   he rejoins his friends.

HATTIE, THE BACKSTAGE BAT   Gr.K-3/$3.50H

Viking, 1970

>   The peccadilloes of a bat who contributes to
>   the action on the stage when a theatre opens.
>   She is, in fact, largely responsible for the play's
>   success.

Gaeddert, Lou Ann
NOISY NANCY AND NICK   PS-3/$4.50L

Doubleday, 1970

> An exploration of the noisy city by Noisy Nancy and Nick, her friend.

NOISY NANCY MORRIS   Gr.PS-1/$3.95L

Doubleday, 1965

> Poor Nancy discovers that even though she has fun making noises, and even though it's creative, her audiences don't always applaud.

Garber, Nancy
AMY'S LONG NIGHT   Gr.K-3

Albert Whitman, 1970

> To celebrate her sixth birthday in real grown-up style, Amy and her dog stay up all night by themselves.

Garelick, May
JUST SUPPOSE   Gr.K-3/$.75P

Scholastic Book Services, 1969

> A lot of supposing is done by both boys and girls who pretend that they are many different animals.

Gauch, Patricia Lee
CHRISTINA KATERINA   Gr.K-3/$4.99L
AND THE BOX

Coward, McCann and Geoghegan, 1971

>   Despite the existence of a stereotypic mother,
>   this story has some value in depicting creative
>   play. Using an empty shipping carton, Christina
>   makes a variety of buildings as well as a racing
>   car.

Gill, Joan
SARA'S GRANNY AND THE GROODLE   Gr.K-3

Doubleday, 1969

>   Sara's granny is a colorful character and,
>   thanks to her, Sara is able to take off on flights
>   of fancy.

Goffstein, M.B.
GOLDIE THE DOLLMAKER   Gr.K-3/$3.50H

Farrar, Straus & Giroux, 1969

>   In this gentle story, the forest provides shelter
>   and working materials for Goldie who supports
>   her simple life by making and selling dolls.

_____

TWO PIANO TUNERS   Gr.PS-3/$3.50H

Farrar, Straus & Giroux

>   Since her grandfather is a piano tuner, and
>   since she admires him a great deal, Debbie
>   decides that she, too, wants to be a piano tuner
>   so she becomes his apprentice.

Goldsmid, Paula
DID YOU EVER?   Gr.PS-K

Lollipop Power, 1971

> A nursery rhyme book which gives children the
> chance to act out the things they think they
> would like to be.

Goodyear, Carmen
THE SHEEP BOOK   Gr.PS-2

Lollipop Power, 1972

> An idyllic setting on a California farm where a
> farmer tends her sheep. It is a story which
> shows sensitivity to the sights and sounds of
> the pastoral life.

Grant, Sandy
HEY, LOOK AT ME!   Gr.PS-1/$4.95H

Bradbury Press, 1973

> There are vibrant action photographs of city
> children, adults, animals in this ABC book.

Greenberg, Polly
OH LORD, I WISH   Gr.K-1/$5.95H
I WAS A BUZZARD

Macmillan, 1968

> The story of a black family in the South whose
> lives revolve largely around the cotton harvest.

Greenburg, Dan
JUMBO THE BOY AND   Gr.2-4/$4.50H
ARNOLD THE ELEPHANT

Bobbs-Merrill, 1969

> A delightful fantasy in which fathers and mothers both share in the confusion attendant upon a nursery's mixing up of a baby boy and a baby elephant.

Greenfield, Eloise
BUBBLES   Gr.PS-4/$2.50P

Drum & Spear Press, 1972

> A black boy entertains his mother as he learns to read; he practices reading to his little sister when his mother is pre-occupied with chores.

Hall, Marie
GILBERTO AND THE WIND   Gr.PS-1/$.95P/$3.00H

Viking, 1967

> The wind has a variety of personalities, Gilberto discovers, when he sails, blows bubbles or flies a kite.

Hill, Elizabeth S.
EVAN'S CORNER   Gr.K-3/$1.45P/$3.95H

Holt, Rinehart & Winston, 1967

> Evan needs a place he can call his and his alone.

Hoban, Russell
BEST FRIENDS FOR FRANCES   Gr.PS-3/$3.95H

Harper & Row, 1969

> How a female badger finds a male badger friend, and how she gets him to make an iron-clad resolution: basketball games which exclude girls are strictly out.

A BIRTHDAY FOR FRANCES   Gr.K-3/$3.95H

Harper & Row, 1968

> How jealousy affects Frances the Badger when her sister has a birthday.

BREAD AND JAM FOR FRANCES   Gr.K-3/$3.95H

Harper & Row, 1964

> More experiences with Frances. This time she is on a meatless diet of bread and jam.

Hochschild, Arlie Russell
COLEEN THE QUESTION GIRL   Gr.1-5/$2.50P

Feminist Press, 1974

> An engaging story of a little girl who has a faculty for asking lots of questions.

Hoffman, Phyllis
STEFFIE AND ME   Gr.1-4/$3.79L

Franklin Watts, 1972

> Girls can be many things they want to be,
> including being strong and independent.

Hopkins, Marjorie
THE THREE VISITORS   Gr.K-3/$4.95H

Parents Magazine Press, 1967

> An Eskimo child's kindness to a trio of visitors
> is rewarded by each giving her a magic present.

Karsilovsky, Phyllis
THE MAN WHO   Gr.K-3/$3.50H
DIDN'T WASH HIS DISHES

Doubleday, 1950

> Coping with the cooking is one hurdle a man
> manages to get over, but doing the dishes
> presents a much worse problem.

Katz, Bobbi
I'LL BUILD MY FRIEND   Gr.K-3/$.95P
A MOUNTAIN

Scholastic Book Services, 1972

> A young boy's fantasy about building his
> friend a mountain of "good stuff" such as toys
> and fruit and summertime snow.

NOTHING BUT A DOG   Gr.K-3/$2.50P

Feminist Press, 1972

>While there are lots of things a child likes to do, and things she would like to have, nothing can stop the longing for a dog.

Keith, Eros
NANCY'S BACK YARD   Gr.PS-3/$4.95H

Harper & Row, 1973

>By acting out their parts, four children exchange fantastic dreams of dragons and of Cinderella, of riding animals and of diving into the sea.

Kesselman, Wendy
ANGELITA   Gr.K-6/$4.95H

Hill & Wang, 1970

>A study in the contrasts of her personality as Angelita leaves her native Puerto Rico for an apartment in New York. Once outgoing and lively, she becomes lonely and morose.

Klein, Norma
A TRAIN FOR JANE   Gr.K-4/$3.50P

Feminist Press, 1974

>Jane is exhorted by parents and others, in rhyme, to want anything from beads to a doll house to a box of chocolates for Christmas.

From *Mary Jo's Grandmother* by Janice May Udry

Her stock reply is "But I want a train." And she gets one.

_____

GIRLS CAN BE ANYTHING   Gr.PS-1/$1.95P/$5.50H

E.P. Dutton, 1973

Stereotypic ideas of girls' prescribed roles are confronted and neatly disposed of in this book where women are shown to become doctors, pilots, politicians.

Krauss, Ruth
A HOLE IS TO DIG   Gr.PS-1/$2.95H

Harper & Row, 1952

In a primer of definitions, boys and girls share all activities together.

Lasker, Joe
MOTHERS CAN DO ANYTHING   Gr.K-3/$4.25H

Albert Whitman, 1972

As the title indicates, mothers are depicted in unusual, as well as traditional, roles.

Laurence
SEYMOURINA   Gr.PS-2/$5.95H

Bobbs-Merrill, 1970

A gentle fantasy about Seymourina's search for the Land of Love which knows no war, and which is like a Garden of Eden.

Leaf, Munro
THE STORY OF FERDINAND   Gr.K-3/$.95P/$2.95H

Viking, 1936

> This early story was very popular a generation ago, and was made into an animated film. Ferdinand is a gentle, easy-going bull who loves to smell flowers and live in peace rather than fight. But despite his passive nature, he has a strong personality.

Lear, Edward
THE STORY OF THE FOUR   Gr.K-3/$3.95H
LITTLE CHILDREN WHO WENT
AROUND THE WORLD

Macmillan, 1967

> A delightful fantasy in which two boys and two girls share exciting adventures.

Lenthall, Patricia Riley
CARLOTTA AND THE SCIENTIST   Gr.K-4/$2.00P

Lollipop Power, 1973

> A mother penguin has some unsettling experiences as she hunts for food for her children.

Lewis, Luevester
JACKIE
                                        Gr.K-5/$1.00P

Third World Press, 1970

> The new kid on the block is actually a girl, but the boys in the neighborhood don't realize it

until school starts and Jackie goes to her first
class wearing a dress.

Lobel, Arnold
LUCILLE   Gr.K-3/$2.95H

Harper & Row, 1964

Lucille, the farmer's plow horse, decides that
she is dull and dirty and wants to be something
else. The farmer and his wife take her to town
and buy her "ladylike" finery. But Lucille
discovers she doesn't want to be a "lady";
"I am glad to be a plain happy horse," she says.

Lorree, Sharron
THE SUNSHINE FAMILY   Gr.PS-2/$4.50H
AND THE PONY

Seabury Press, 1972

A group of friends make the big transition
from city to country life.

Matsuno, Masako
A PAIR OF RED CLOGS   Gr.K-3/$4.91L

Collins & World, 1960

The clogs remind grandmother of her youth
and of how they were a part of games she
played with her friends.

Matsutani, Miyoko
THE WITCH'S MAGIC CLOTH   Gr.K-3/$4.95H

Parents Magazine Press, 1969

>An old Japanese folk tale in which only
>Grandma Asaka is brave enough not to fear the
>witch.

Mayer, Mercer
THE QUEEN ALWAYS   Gr.PS-2/$5.29L
WANTED TO DANCE

Simon and Schuster, 1971

>A free-wheeling Queen who wants to do what
>she wants to do, and a King who passes laws
>against her doing them. First her dancing
>upsets some people, so the dance is outlawed;
>when she sings, the King outlaws singing.

McCloskey, Robert
BLUEBERRIES FOR SAL   Gr.PS-1/$.95P

Viking, 1948

>Role reversals, but involving two different
>species of animal, as a bear cub and a little girl
>unwittingly exchange mothers.

———————

ONE MORNING IN MAINE   Gr.PS-3/$.95P/$5.95H

Viking, 1952

>The salty adventures of Sal who lives with her
>family on an island off the coast of Maine. She
>has a multitude of experiences, which include a

conversation with a seal, as well as activities
with her father.

Merriam, Eve
BOYS AND GIRLS,   Gr.PS-3/$1.65P/$4.95L
GIRLS AND BOYS

Holt, Rinehart & Winston, 1972

Children of varying ethnic backgrounds play in
an atmosphere free of sexual stereotypes.

MOMMIES AT WORK   Gr.K-2/$.95P

Scholastic Book Services, 1971

Mommies are shown doing many jobs which
are traditionally considered to be jobs for
daddies. They work on assembly lines and are
engineers as well as secretaries.

Merrill, Jean and Scott, Frances
HOW MANY KIDS ARE   Gr.1-3/$3.95L
HIDING ON MY BLOCK?

Albert Whitman, 1970

A game of hide and seek with many different
boys and girls.

Minard, Rosemary, Ed.
WOMENFOLK AND FAIRY TALES   Gr.1-5/$5.95H

Houghton Mifflin, 1975

Although many fairy tales are blatantly sexist,
the editor of this collection has chosen a group

which are not, and which can be enjoyed by both boys and girls. Heroines are heroic, even though some end by marrying, "a tacked-on ending typical of much early literature," the editor says.

Myers, Walter D.
THE DANCERS   Gr.K-3/$4.95H

Parents Magazine Press, 1972

When a ballerina comes to dance with some of his friends, a black boy gets a chance to meet her.

Ness, Evaline
DO YOU HAVE   Gr.K-3/$1.25P/$5.50H
THE TIME, LYDIA?

E.P. Dutton & Co., 1971

Lydia learns to budget her time more efficiently after she leaves a number of her activities unfinished.

––––––––

SAM, BANGS AND   Gr.PS-2/$1.45P/$4.50H
MOONSHINE

Holt, Rinehart & Winston, 1966

"Moonshine" is what Samantha's father calls her for telling fish stories. Caldecott Medal Winner.

Ormsby, Virginia
TWENTY-ONE CHILDREN   Gr.PS-3/$3.95H
PLUS TEN

Lippincott, 1971

> An insight into the complications which arise
> when a school is integrated for the first time.

Paxton, Tom
JENNIFER'S RABBIT   Gr.PS-3/$1.75L

Putnam, 1970

> Folk singer Paxton has provided the story as
> well as the music for a charming fantasy about
> Jennifer and her assortment of animal friends
> who dance and play with sailors aboard ship.

Phillips, Lynn
EXACTLY LIKE ME   Gr.PS-3/$1.75L

Lollipop Power, 1972

> A resourceful and self-confident girl is anxious
> to become an adult so she can prove what
> women can really be.

Phleger, Frederick
ANN CAN FLY   Gr.1-2/$2.95H

Random House, 1959

> In this Beginner Book, Ann's father starts
> teaching her to fly an airplane, and even urges
> her to take over the controls.

Plenn, Doris
THE VIOLET TREE   Gr.1-5

Farrar, Straus & Giroux, 1962

> A rooster in San Juan, who is supposed to be a
> fighter, rejects the violence he detests, and,
> with the aid of a brave hen, flees the city.

Politi, Leo
MOY MOY   Gr.PS-3/$5.95L

Scribner, 1960

> The Chinese New Year is celebrated by Moy
> Moy and her brothers.

Preston, Edna Mitchell
HORRIBLE HEPZIBAH   Gr.K-3/$3.50H

Viking, 1971

> Despite — or perhaps because of — her can-
> tankerous ways, Hepzibah's way prevails in a
> book that contains both humor and irony.

THE TEMPER TANTRUM BOOK   Gr.K-2/$.95P/$4.50H

Viking, 1969

> By exercising the spirit, the body and the vocal
> chords, Elizabeth and Lionel, elephant and lion
> respectively, act out some of the frustrations
> suffered by little children.

Reavin, Sam
HURRAH FOR CAPTAIN JANE!   Gr.K-3/$4.95H

Parents Magazine Press, 1971

>Jane indulges herself in some venturesome
>wish-fulfillment as the first woman captain of
>an ocean-going passenger vessel . . . all in her
>bathtub.

Ross, Pat
HI FLY   Gr.K-3/$3.50L

Crown, 1971

>There's nothing like being a fly on the wall to
>get a very special perspective on things. The
>heroine of this picture book is reduced to the
>size of a fly, and, with a fly friend, has some
>hair-raising adventures.

Sandberg, Inger and Lasse
WHAT LITTLE ANNA SAVED   Gr.PS-2/$3.95

Lothrop, Lee & Shepard, 1965

>Little Anna is a most resourceful and imagina-
>tive young girl. Things that most people might
>consider trash or castoffs Anna turns into
>useful objects.

Schick, Eleanor
CITY IN THE WINTER   Gr.K-3/$.95P/$5.95H

Collier, 1972

>Though his mother is still able to go to work
>during a blizzard, Jimmy's school is closed for
>the day; he and his grandmother busy them-

selves with making soup, feeding the birds and other fun things.

Schweitzer, Byrd
AMIGO   Gr.K-3/$.95P/$5.95H

Collier, 1963

A boy and a prairie dog adopt each other and become the best of friends.

Scott, Ann H.
ON MOTHER'S LAP   Gr.K-3/$4.95H

McGraw-Hill, 1972

An Eskimo boy finds a comfortable world for himself and his possessions on his mother's lap.

Segal, Lore
TELL ME A MITZI   Gr.K-3/$4.95H

Farrar, Straus & Giroux, 1970

There are three stories about her family life as told by Mitzi, involving a variety of humorous situations.

Sharmat, Marjorie W.
GLADYS TOLD ME   Gr.PS-3/$4.79L
TO MEET HER HERE

Harper & Row, 1970

Gladys is Irving's friend, and he recalls the fun they had together as he goes looking for her at the zoo.

Shulevitz, Uri
RAIN RAIN RIVERS   Gr.K-3/$4.95H

Farrar, Straus & Giroux, 1969

> As the rain falls, a little girl takes imaginative
> journeys to other places where puddles will be
> her playground.

Simon, Norma
I WAS SO MAD!   Gr.K-2/$4.25H

Albert Whitman, 1974

> Several boys and girls tell what makes them
> mad, and, by so doing, open up the way for
> readers to deal with their own anger. There is a
> song at the end of the book entitled "There
> Was a Man and He Was Mad" whose anger costs
> him dear.

Sonneborn, Ruth
I LOVE GRAM   Gr.K-3/$3.75H

Viking, 1971

> Both mother and grandmother in this black
> family work and head the household. When her
> grandmother is taken to the hospital, Sallie is
> afraid that the old woman will not survive the
> ordeal.

Surowecki, Sandra
JOSHUA'S DAY   Gr.PS-1

Lollipop Power, 1972

> Joshua lives in a home without a father, and his

photographer-mother takes him to a day care center every day, a wholesome environment in which he can grow and learn.

Tallon, Robert
THE THING IN DOLORES' PIANO   Gr.1-4/$5.95H

Bobbs-Merrill, 1970

"The Thing", whatever it is, makes other-worldly noises in an attempt to put Dolores off.

Taylor, Mark
A TIME FOR FLOWERS   Gr.K-3/$4.64L

Golden Gate Junior Books, 1967

Equality of brother and sister are most note-worthy in this picture of Japanese-Americans. The story involves the children's unexpected adventures as they set out selling flowers to raise enough money to replace their grand-father's broken glasses.

Thayer, Jane
QUIET ON ACCOUNT   Gr.K-3/$4.64L
OF DINOSAUR

Morrow, 1964

A little girl who happens to find a dinosaur decides to take it to school. She grows up to become a renowned scientist because, natur-ally, she knows more about dinosaurs than anyone else in the world.

Thomas, Ianthe
LORDY, AUNT HATTIE   Gr.PS-3/$4.95H

Harper & Row, 1973

Summer time is a time of discovery for Jeppa
Lee, a black girl who spends the season with
her aunt.

Uchida, Yoshiko
SUMI AND THE GOAT   Gr.K-4/$4.50H
AND THE TOKYO EXPRESS

Miki the goat, by simply grazing along the railroad tracks, immobilizes the Tokyo Express.
This gives all the children in Sumi's village a
chance to tour the train.

Udry, Janice May
MARY JO'S GRANDMOTHER   Gr.K-3/$4.25H

Albert Whitman, 1972

A pleasant story about a little black girl who
behaves bravely during a crisis in her grandmother's life.

———————

WHAT MARY JO SHARED   Gr.K-2/$4.25H

Albert Whitman, 1966

Mary Jo, a little black girl, is very shy: she
would like to bring something to school to
share with her class, but she is afraid to try.

Besides, other children keep showing the things she wants to bring. Mary Jo finally thinks of something no one else has ever thought of bringing.

WHAT MARY JO WANTED   Gr.K-3/$3.95H

Albert Whitman, 1968

The story of a little black girl and the love of her puppy.

Van Woerkom, Dorothy
THE QUEEN WHO   Gr.K-3/$5.50H
COULDN'T BAKE GINGERBREAD

Knopf, 1975

A funny story, with illustrations to match, about a King and his new Queen who have made mutually compromised choices. She cannot bake gingerbread, as he had wanted in a wife, and he cannot play the slide trombone, as she had wanted in a husband. But all ends well as the King learns to bake gingerbread and the Queen to play the slide trombone.

Waber, Bernard
IRA SLEEPS OVER   Gr.K-3/$4.95H

Houghton Mifflin, 1972

Ira struggles with a momentous decision: should he or should he not take along his teddy bear when he goes to his friend's house for the first time to spend the night?

Wahl, Jan
A WOLF OF MY OWN   Gr.K-2/$4.95H

Macmillan, 1969

> Fred is the name of the puppy a little girl receives as a birthday gift, but she prefers to refer to it as her "wolf friend."

Wellman, Alice W.
TATU AND THE HONEY BIRD   Gr.K-3/$3.96L

Putnam, 1972

> Tatu and his sister, West African children, are determined to go to school together despite the opposition of their grandmother who pooh-poohs the idea of a girl getting an education.

Wells, Rosemary
NOISY NORA   Gr.PS-1/$4.95H

Dial Press, 1973

> Here we have the problem of sibling rivalry, its attendant anger and how to deal with it, as Nora, the middle mouse child, runs away from home because she thinks her parents care more about their other children than about her.

Wikland, Ilon
I CAN HELP TOO!   Gr.PS/$1.50H

Random House, 1974

> A little boy is pictured scrubbing a floor, washing dishes, sewing and doing various other domestic tasks usually thought of as being performed exclusively by little girls.

Williams, Jay
THE PRACTICAL PRINCESS   Gr.K-3/$4.95H

Parents Magazine Press, 1973

> An amusing rescue story with traditional roles
> turned around: the prince is rescued by the
> princess.

PETRONELLA   Gr.K-3/$4.95H

Parents Magazine Press, 1973

> A clever reversal of roles as Petronella sallies
> forth to find fame, fortune and a prince. It all
> adds up to good adventure as the heroine dis-
> plays both courage and kindness.

THE SILVER WHISTLE   Gr.1-3/$4.95H

Parents Magazine Press, 1971

> It takes the daughter of a wise old woman to
> have the courage and gusto to seek her own
> fortune, as Prudence does.

Wolde, Gunilla
TOMMY AND SARAH DRESS UP   Gr.PS/$1.25P

Houghton Mifflin, 1972

> A boy and a girl dress up as adults; once as
> men, on another occasion as women.

TOMMY GOES TO THE DOCTOR   Gr.PS/$1.25P

Houghton Mifflin, 1972

> Tommy watches in fascination as his doctor uses her instruments to examine him. He repeats the performance with Teddy Bear as his patient.

Yashima, Taro
CROW BOY   Gr.1-6/$.95P

Viking, 1955

> After suffering six years of mockery by his grade schoolmates, Chibi is finally appreciated by a teacher who discovers the boy's genuine individuality.

UMBRELLA   Gr.PS-1/$.95P/$3.50H

Viking, 1958

> With the unbrella goes a pair of red boots, birthday gifts which Momo wears to her nursery school one day when it is raining.

Yolen, Jane
THE WITCH WHO WASN'T   Gr.1-3/$1.25P/$5.95H

Macmillan, 1964

> Being different, as Isabel is in her own witch family, involves the same kinds of complications for her as it does for ordinary mortals.

Young, Miriam
JELLYBEANS FOR BREAKFAST   Gr.K-3/$4.95H

Parents Magazine Press, 1968

> The fantasies shared by two little girls who plan all sorts of things they will do one day, including a trip to the moon.

Zolotow, Charlotte
WILLIAM'S DOLL   Gr.PS-3/$4.95H

Harper & Row, 1972

> Grandma teaches William's father an important lesson: if he allows him to have the doll he wants, his son will be a better person and, consequently, will make a better father.

PRE-SCHOOL THROUGH THIRD GRADE

NON-FICTION

Graff, Stewart and Polly Anne
HELEN KELLER: TOWARD   Gr.1-4/$3.40H
THE LIGHT

Garrard, 1965

> A book about Helen Keller's life with Anne
> Sullivan Macy, her teacher.

Hollander, Phyllis
AMERICAN WOMEN IN SPORTS   Gr.PS-3

Grossett & Dunlap, 1972

> In a male-dominated world, competitiveness is
> generally not considered a female character-
> istic; this book tells the story of a dozen
> accomplished women athletes who achieved
> pre-eminence in a field dominated by men.

Jordan, Jane
FANNIE LOU HAMER   Gr.1-5/$1.25/$4.50H

Crowell, 1972

> A picture-biography of one of America's most
> dynamic civil rights leaders. Among her
> activities are included the voter registration
> drive in the south and her work on behalf of
> farm cooperatives.

Lawrence, Jacob
HARRIET AND THE   Gr.1-5/$5.95H
PROMISED LAND

Simon & Schuster, 1968

> Harriet Tubman was a major participant in the campaign smuggling slaves out of the south.

Levenson, Dorothy
WOMEN OF THE WEST   Gr.1-5/$4.50H

Franklin Watts, 1973

> An examination of the role played by women on the frontier. Black, Indian and white women are dealt with; women are seen as workers, teachers, outlaws, rights activists, prohibitionists, and in many other roles. Bibliography, index, many illustrations and photographs.

Rockwell, Harlow
MY DOCTOR   Gr.PS-2/$4.95H

Macmillan, 1973

> An explanation, with pictures, of the instruments a doctor uses when she examines people.

Tobias, Tobi
MARIAN ANDERSON   Gr.1-5/$3.95H

Crowell, 1972

> One of America's best known singers first had to achieve a measure of fame in Europe before her own country recognized her talent.

We climb ladders,
we sew dresses,
we make music,
we make messes.

We can do all these things,
you see,
whether we are he or she.

From *He Bear She Bear* by Stan and Jan Berenstain

Chapter Two

Third Grade through Seventh Grade

From *Nine Lives of Moses* by Marion Fuller Archer

FICTION

Abramovitz, Anita
WINIFRED   Gr.3-7/$3.75H

Steck-Vaughn, 1971

> A clever, charming story about Winifred and
> her sign painting business which seems to upset
> her neighbors. But she forges ahead in spite of
> the difficulties, although she does make some
> adjustments in her way of doing business.

Aiken, Joan
THE CUCKOO TREE   Gr.3-7/$4.95H

Doubleday, 1971

> Smugglers, intrigue, heroism all combine in a
> story about Dido Twite who saves King Jamie
> from the Hanovers whose insidious plot was
> designed to disrupt the King's coronation.

Archer, Marion Fuller
NINE LIVES OF MOSES   Gr.5-7/$4.25H

Albert Whitman, 1968

> A little girl named Charlotte protects her black
> cat as she travels with her family from Wiscon-
> sin to Oregon in 1852.

Bailey, Carolyn S.
MISS HICKORY   Gr.4-7/$4.50H

Viking, 1946

> The winter trials and tribulations of a scare-
> crow who meets a wide variety of animals,
> some friendly, some hostile. Among others are
> a depressed hen-pheasant and Mr. T. Willard
> Brown, a barn cat with a reputation as a
> hunter.

Bawden, Nina
THE RUNAWAY SUMMER   Gr.4-7/$4.75H

Lippincott, 1969

> An illegal alien named Krishna meets two
> friendly youngsters, Mary and Simon, who try
> to help him out of his assorted difficulties.

Beatty, Patricia
HAIL COLUMBIA   Gr.5-9/$6.95L

Morrow, 1970

> This story takes place in the early 1900's in the
> upper northwestern United States where a suf-
> fragist and her niece share a series of strange
> experiences.

———————

RED ROCK OVER THE RIVER   Gr.4-7/$5.49H

Morrow, 1973

> An exciting action Western with a neat twist:

this time the fastest gun around is a woman, and one who is half Indian as well.

Blue, Rose
GRANDMA DIDN'T WAVE BACK   Gr.3-5/$4.90L

Franklin Watts, 1972

When her Grandmother, who lives with her and her parents, begins to fail, Debbie is upset at the idea of change as it confronts her for the first time.

THE PREACHER'S KID   Gr.4-6/$5.95H

Franklin Watts, 1975

Linda, a minister's daughter, is forced to think carefully about her father's actions and her own attitudes toward him, toward her friends, and toward society in general when the issue of busing black children to the white school erupts in their small town.

Blume, Judy
BLUBBER   Gr.3+/$5.95H

Bradbury Press, 1974

Jill Brenner, who tells the story, is in the fifth grade. Wendy, the class bully, decides that Linda, who is rather plump, should be nicknamed Blubber because she gave a report on whales. This is the beginning of Wendy's campaign to torment Linda, in which Jill and the whole class join. But Wendy is dangerous and unpredictable, and Jill herself eventually learns what it feels like to be persecuted. She finds that it is important not to let other people decide what is going to happen to you: passivity can be destructive.

IGGIE'S HOUSE   Gr.4-7/$5.95H

Bradbury Press, 1970

Iggie, Winnie's friend, had to move to Tokyo, and new people have bought his family's house. The Garbers, the new owners, are black, and Winnie is excited about their moving in, but puzzled at the Garbers' suspicion of her enthusiasm. She is also confused that her mother's reaction to Mrs. Landon's efforts at running the Garbers out of the neighborhood is not more violent. Winnie discovers life is more complicated than she had thought.

Bremer, Barbara
A YEAR IN THE LIFE   Gr.5+
OF ROSIE BERNARD

Harper & Row, 1971

The year takes place in Brooklyn in the 1830's when Rosie is ten. She decides then that she will be a doctor, even as she struggles with adjusting to her father's new marriage and her own cultural mixture of Protestant and Jew.

Brill, Ethel C.
MADELEINE TAKES COMMAND   Gr.4-6

McGraw-Hill, 1946

> Madeleine becomes commander during the defense of a fort being attacked by the Iroquois in Canada.

Brink, Carole R.
BABY ISLAND   Gr.4-7/$.95P/$4.95H

Macmillan, 1937

> Four babies are rescued by Jean and Murray Wallace when the ocean liner on which they are sailing sinks and they take refuge on an island.

Burch, Robert
QUEENIE PEAVY   Gr.3-7/$4.50H

Viking, 1966

> How Queenie learns to leaven her obstinacy with benign feelings when her troubles deepen. Even more important, she learns to believe in herself.

Burnett, Francis Hodgson
THE SECRET GARDEN   Gr.3-7/$6.50H

Lippincott, 1911

> A stubborn and self-willed young girl learns that there are genuine rewards when one feels for others.

Burton, Hester
TIME OF TRIAL   Gr.5-9/$5.91L

Collins & World, 1964

As an atypical 19th century English woman,
Margaret is a rugged individualist who shares
her father's active liberalism.

Canfield, Dorothy
UNDERSTOOD BETSY   Gr.4-7/$.60P

Holt, Rinehart & Winston, 1916

After living a cosseted life with her aunts,
Betsy is coaxed into independence and individuality when she moves to a farm owned by
some other relatives.

Clark, Ann N.
ALONG SANDY TRAILS   Gr.4-6/$5.95H

Viking, 1969

A gentle story of how an Indian, along with her
grandmother, explores the beauty of the
desert. Photographs.

Cleaver, Vera and Bill
ELLEN GRAE   Gr.4-7/$4.75H

Lippincott, 1967

Like the boy who cried wolf, Ellen is a congen-
ital teller of fish stories, and when she finally
tells the truth for once, she is disbelieved. The
consequences are both funny and serious.

LADY ELLEN GRAE   Gr.4-7/$3.95H

Lippincott, 1968

Becoming a "lady" requires Ellen's resettle-
ment to Seattle. Her cousin Laura and her aunt
Eleanor teach her to become "sophisticated,"
but in the end she goes home to rural Florida.

THE MIMOSA TREE   Gr.4-7/$3.95H

Lippincott, 1970

An Appalachian family's struggle for survival
'midst urban decay finds teenaged Marvella
Profitt assuming a leadership role.

WHERE THE LILLIES BLOOM   Gr.4-7/$4.95H

Lippincott, 1969

Another story of Appalachian heroism as four-
teen-year-old Mary Call leads her abandoned,
impoverished family out of destitution and
despair after the death of her father, which she
must conceal in order to keep them all
together.

Clymer, Eleanor
THE SPIDER, THE CAVE   Gr.3-7/$4.95
AND THE POTTERY BOWL

Atheneum, 1971

> The story of an American Indian girl is full of
> adventure in which she has a number of close
> calls.

Colver, Anne
BORROWED TREASURE   Gr.3-5/$4.99H

Knopf, 1959

> There is a mystery involving an animal they
> very much want, so Molly-O and Pip solve it
> together.

_____

SECRET CASTLE   Gr.3-5/$4.99H

Knopf, 1961

> Another Molly-O and Pip adventure finds the
> pair on a trip to the Thousand Islands where
> they uncover a new mystery.

Conford, Ellen
DREAMS OF VICTORY   Gr.4-6/$4.95H

Little Brown, 1973

> Dreams, for Victory Banneker, are much more
> pleasant than reality. In dreams she is wildly
> successful in a variety of roles, but in reality is
> a failure. She manages to attain a measure of
> success in real life, after all.

Constant, Alberta Wilson
THE MOTORING MILLERS   Gr.3-7/$5.95H

Crowell, 1969

> The Millers, a unique clan, include a daughter
> who becomes a winning racing car driver.

Coolidge, Olivia
COME BY HERE   Gr.5-8/$4.95H

Houghton Mifflin, 1970

> Set in the early part of the 20th century is the
> story of an orphaned black child who must
> learn to cope with the harshness and uncer-
> tainty of a difficult and lonely life.

Corcoran, Barbara
THE LONG JOURNEY   Gr.4-6/$1.25P/$5.50H

Atheneum, 1970

> Laurie must be brave and self-reliant as she
> rides from the defunct mining town which was
> her home to a new life in Butte, Montana.

Dalgliesh, Alice
THE SILVER PENCIL   Gr.3-7

Scribner, 1944

> The literary aspirations of a budding young
> author whose first book is published after her
> experiences here and abroad are told.

Dickinson, Peter
THE DEVIL'S CHILDREN   Gr.4-6/$5.95H

Little, Brown, 1970

> There are superstition and inexplicable forces
> at work in this lusty adventure story about
> Nicky Gore. She challenges the supernatural,
> placates the fears of villagers, and intercedes on
> behalf of a nomadic tribe. All this occurs as she
> attempts to wend her way to France to join her
> family.

––––––––––

EMMA TUPPER'S DIARY   Gr.4-6/$5.95H

Little, Brown, 1972

> While on a holiday in the Highlands, which she
> thought was going to be a tranquil one, Emma
> Tupper is threatened with danger. But because
> of her ingenuity and common sense, she is able
> to elude harm.

Enright, Elizabeth
THIMBLE SUMMER   Gr.4-6/$4.95H

Holt, Rinehart & Winston, 1938

> The wholesome, down-home experiences of a
> young girl on a farm in the 1930's. The lively
> heroine has a variety of adventures, both on
> and off the farm. Newbery Medal Winner.

ZEEE   Gr.3-7/$5.50H

Harcourt Brace Jovanovich, 1965

> The villains of the piece are People, and the
> victim is an intriguing fairy named Zeee whose
> personal possessions are destroyed by Mortals.
> But a young girl saves her in the nick of time.

Fall, Thomas
DANDY'S MOUNTAIN   Gr.3-7/$5.95H

Dial Press, 1967

> Dandy is an engaging character with a dynamic
> working mother. Dandy herself, in planning her
> summer, encounters the unexpected as she
> retrieves an obstreperous young cousin from
> Mt. Everest.

Farley, Walter
THE BLACK STALLION   Gr.4+/$2.95H
AND THE GIRL

Random House, 1971

> Because racing, like most enterprises, has been
> confined mostly to males, horsewoman Pam is
> confronted by some opposition when she tries
> to break into the field. "Racing is a rough
> business; it's not for girls," says Henry Dailey,
> Black Stallion's trainer. But Pam's will and
> determination prove otherwise.

Fitzhugh, Louise
HARRIET THE SPY   Gr.4-7/$1.25P

Harper & Row, 1964

There is nothing ordinary about Harriet who is
convinced that in order to be a great writer she
must write down all details about people's
lives. While that is not the kind of activity
which tends to endear her to everyone's heart,
Harriet is nonetheless an appealing character.

Freeman, Barbara C.
LUCINDA   Gr.3-7

Grosset & Dunlap, 1967

A 19th century child has the audacity to chal-
lenge the despotism of her rich, penny-pinching
uncle Prescott who is also her guardian. Their
relationship ends, but it's only the beginning of
Lucinda's trials.

Gauch, Patricia Lee
THIS TIME, TEMPE WICK?   Gr.3-7/$5.95H

Coward, McCann & Geoghegan, 1974

A fictionalized story of a spirited and interesting historical character named Temperence
Wick and of her adventures during the Revol-
utionary War in New Jersey. Not only is she
physically strong and a first rate horsewoman,
but she also becomes more than a match for
two Pennsylvania soldiers who try to steal her
horse, Bonny.

Godden, Rumer
THE DOLLS' HOUSE   Gr.3-7/$5.95H

Viking, 1948

> A study in contrasts takes place in a Victorian
> doll house. Some of the inhabitants feel them-
> selves grand and elegant, while unpretentious
> Tottie remembers very well that part of her
> used to be a tree.

Greene, Constance C.
LEO THE LIONESS   Gr.5-9/$.95P

Viking, 1970

> As she begins to ask questions about standards
> of behavior, Tibb discovers the harsh truth that
> reality falls somewhat short of the ideal.

Gripe, Maria
THE NIGHT DADDY   Gr.3-7/$4.50H

Delacorte, 1971

> A working mother leaves her daughter in the
> care of an unusual young man.

Hamilton, Virginia
ZEELY   Gr.5-9/$1.25P/$5.95H

Macmillan, 1967

> Zeely, a lonely and wise woman, helps an
> eleven-year-old black girl through the transition
> from fantasy to reality.

Hart, Carole
DELILAH   Gr.2-6/$3.95H

Harper & Row, 1973

> Delilah is at the age when she begins to com-
> prehend adult emotions. She is a young girl
> who will clearly go her own way, and will not
> be intimidated by others' expectations.

Hautzig, Esther
THE ENDLESS STEPPE   Gr.5-7/$4.50H

Crowell, 1968

> In 1940, the Russians take a Jewish family
> from their home in Poland and resettle them in
> Siberia where they face a life of deprivation.

Hull, Katharine & Whitlock, Pamela
FAR DISTANT OXUS   Gr.5-8/$4.95H

Macmillan, (abridged) 1969

> Two English schoolgirls wrote this story about
> the adventures of girls and boys in which both
> sexes exhibit courage, resourcefulness and
> daring.

Jackson, Jacqueline
MISSING MELINDA   Gr.4-7/$4.95H

Little, Brown, 1967

> An antique doll of great value is found by
> twins Cordelia and Ophelia, only to suddenly
> disappear again in a maze of intrigue. The story
> is told alternately by the two sisters.

THE PALEFACE REDSKINS   Gr.4-7

Little, Brown, 1958

> A make-believe war is initiated by summer play-Indians. Their target is a group of boy scouts they single out as the Paleface enemy.

THE TASTE OF SPRUCE GUM   Gr.4-7/$4.95

Little, Brown, 1966

> A mother and daughter move to a lumber camp in Vermont in the early 1900's where they find a life of hardship, and where Libby Fletcher finds her new stepfather less than endearing.

Katz, Bobbi
THE MANIFESTO   Gr.3-7/$.95P/$4.95
AND ME — MEG

Franklin Watts, 1974

> Sixth-grader Meg Prescott decides that consciousness-raising should begin before adulthood, so she forms a group called The Saturday Sisters who issue a set of principles. This "manifesto" includes the statement "We proclaim girls to be human beings, not decorations!" The impact on the community is considerably greater than Meg anticipates.

ROD-AND-REEL TROUBLE   Gr.3-5/$3.50H

Albert Whitman, 1974

>Lori Davis enters a fishing contest which is sponsored annually by the Chicken Thieves Detectives. For the first time the contest does not specify "For Boys Only", and Lori not only wins one of the prizes, but is made "an honorable Chicken Thieves Detective" as well.

Konigsburg, E.L.
FROM THE   Gr.4-7/$1.50P/$6.95H
MIXED-UP FILES OF
MRS. BASIL E. FRANK-WEILER

Atheneum, 1967

>Claudia takes the initiative in devising a plan for herself and her brother to escape from their house in the suburbs to the Metropolitan Museum in New York. Newbery medal winner.

JENNIFER, HECATE,   Gr.3-6/$.95P/$5.25H
MACBETH, WILLIAM MC KINLEY,
AND ME, ELIZABETH

Atheneum, 1967

>A brief foray into witchcraft by Jennifer and Elizabeth ends abruptly when something rather disturbing happens.

A PROUD TASTE FOR SCARLET AND MINIVER

Gr.3-7/$6.95H

Atheneum, 1974

>Eleanor of Aquitaine was one of the great women of history. Not only was she the wife of two kings and the mother of two others, but she was also an unusually dynamic person and a great patron of the arts. In this fictionalized account, each of four people who knew her tells his or her tale.

Krementz, Jill
SWEET PEA

Gr.3-8/$5.95H

Harcourt Brace Jovanovich, 1969

>The scene is set in the rural South; the story is about a young black girl and is told in photographs.

L'Engle, Madeleine
A WRINKLE IN TIME

Gr.3-7/$5.95H

Farrar, Straus & Giroux, 1962

>A hazardous adventure in space where three magic powers named Mrs. Whatsit, Mrs. Which and Mrs. Who weave their mysterious influences. Newbery Medal winner.

Lengstrad, Rolf and Rolen, Pierre L.
THE LONG PONY RACE   Gr.5-7

Knopf, 1966

> In Sweden, where the Long Pony Race is run,
> Fia rides her own pony to a breathtaking win.

Lenski, Lois
JUDY'S JOURNEY   Gr.3-7/$7.95H

Lippincott, 1947

> Judy is a strong heroine and a much-needed
> stabilizing influence on her family who are
> migrant workers travelling from harvest to
> harvest.

STRAWBERRY GIRL   Gr.4-7/$5.95H

Lippincott, 1949

> The difficult life in rural Florida in the 1930's
> where a resourceful girl helps make the best of
> bad circumstances. Newbery Medal winner.

Levitin, Sonia
JOURNEY TO AMERICA   Gr.4-8/$.95P/$4.25H

Atheneum, 1970

> Adult responsibilities are thrust upon Lisa
> when her fatherless family escapes from the
> Nazis and emigrates to America.

RITA, THE WEEKEND RAT   Gr.4-7/$4.50H

Atheneum, 1971

> Cynthia, who is in second grade, has organized a Boy's Club, of which she is the only female member, and from which the boys constantly threaten to expel her. She adopts a pet rat and makes friends with girls, learning what real bravery is all about.

Lewis, C.S.
THE LION, THE WITCH   Gr.4-8/$1.25P/$5.95H
AND THE WARDROBE

Macmillan, 1951

> Heroism is shared equally by two girls and two boys in the first "Narnian Chronicle." Their beloved kingdom is threatened from without by the White Witch, the personificaton of evil. But the forces of Good ultimately triumph.

Lexau, Joan M.
STRIPED ICE CREAM   Gr.3-6/$4.95H

Lippincott, 1968

> A good feeling is shared by a working black mother and her children as one of them is given a surprise birthday party.

Lindgren, Astrid
PIPPI LONGSTOCKING   Gr.3-7/$.95P

Viking, 1950

> This originally Swedish tale involves the adven-
> tures of an unusual heroine named Pippi, an
> amusing and free-wheeling young girl.

Lorenzo, Carol Lee
HEART-OF-SNOWBIRD   Gr.3+/$5.95H

Harper & Row, 1975

> Laurel Ivy lives in Snowbird Gap, a small
> Southern mountain town, with her sister, her
> father, who is a grocer, and his second wife.
> She wants to leave Snowbird Gap as soon as
> she is old enough, go to the city and become a
> dental hygienist. When an Indian family moves
> to town, Laurel befriends Hank Bearfoot, the
> son of an engineer. As a result of this friend-
> ship, her friendship with Judith as well as her
> stepmother's death, she decides to stay and
> learn to be a soil and crop expert for the
> government.

Lystad, Mary
MILLIE THE MONSTER   Gr.2-5/$3.86L

Dial, 1973

> Millie is far from a complacent child as she
> turns from passivity to aggressiveness, and is
> suddenly menacing to friends and family alike.

Miles, Betty
THE REAL ME   Gr.3+/$4.95H

Knopf, 1974

> Barbara Fisher is an independent and self-assertive eleven-year-old who takes over her brother Richard's paper route despite the fact that she encounters hazards and hostilities as a result. The experience opens her eyes to other kinds of role-playing that go on in and out of school.

Molnar, Joe
GRACIELA, A MEXICAN-AMERICAN   Gr.4-7/$4.90L
CHILD TELLS HER STORY

Franklin Watts, 1972

> The peregrinations of a Mexican mining family who travel to Michigan every year from their home in Texas.

Montgomery, L.M.
ANNE OF GREEN GABLES   Gr.5-9/$3.99L

Grosset & Dunlap, 1935

> Prince Edward Island is the setting of this perennial favorite in which Anne, an orphan child, is sent to live with two brothers and their elderly sister, even though they had requested a boy.

Nichols, Ruth
A WALK OUT OF THE WORLD   Gr.4-7/$5.95H

Harcourt Brace Jovanovich, 1969

>On a journey of her mind, Susan travels to an outer world where she finds herself a member of a royal household.

Norris, Gunilla
A FEAST OF LIGHT   Gr.4-7/$4.99H

Knopf, 1967

>Some of the difficult problems a young Swedish girl encounters when she moves to America from her native land.

North, Joan
THE CLOUD FOREST   Gr.6-9/$3.95H

Farrar, Straus & Giroux, 1965

>An energetic young girl who cannot seem to adjust to school shares some weird experiences with her twelve-year-old boy friend.

Norton, Mary
THE BORROWERS   Gr.3-7/$1.95/$5.50H

Harcourt Brace Jovanovich, 1952

>Big people house little people; consequently, little people function as "borrowers," big people as "lenders."

O'Brien, Robert
MRS. FRISBY   Gr.4-6/$1.95P/$6.95H
AND THE RATS OF NIMH

Atheneum, 1971

>   A sad day in the life of a brave mouse: how the
>   widowed Mrs. Frisby rebuilds her family's
>   broken life after they suffer misfortune.

———————

THE SILVER CROWN   Gr.4-7/$.95P/$4.95H

Atheneum, 1968

>   The silver crown is the prize Ellen searches for
>   as she is pursued in her quest by menacing
>   strangers.

O'Dell, Scott
ISLAND OF THE BLUE DOLPHINS   Gr.3-7/$3.95H

Houghton Mifflin, 1960

>   For nearly twenty years, a brave Indian girl
>   lives on a desolate island. She must of necessity
>   be self-reliant and unusually resourceful. New-
>   bery Medal winner.

Orgel, Doris
BARTHOLEMEW, WE LOVE YOU!   Gr.2-5/$4.50H

Knopf, 1973

>   A story which looks at sibling rivalry as it oper-
>   ates between Emily and Kim. But as each
>   focuses her love on a kitten, they begin to

understand that they share other things in common as well.

CINDY'S SAD AND HAPPY TREES   Gr.3-5/$4.99H

Knopf, 1967

A child, heartbroken when she loses her favorite tree, finally comes to grips with reality and chooses another favorite tree.

THE MULBERRY MUSIC   Gr.4-7/$3.95H

Knopf, 1971

Many human tensions and anxieties are dealt with in this story of a young girl and her grandmother. Her grandmother's death seems irrational to Libby, but she must struggle with its reality.

Ormsby, Virginia
MOUNTAIN MAGIC FOR ROSY   Gr.3-7

Crown, 1969

Sibling rivalry rears its ugly head when Rosy is interrupted by her ill baby sister more often than Rosy thinks is bearable.

Pevsner, Stella
BREAK A LEG   Gr.4-9

Crown, 1969

> Some consciousness raising takes place in a
> theater setting as a new-found friend shows
> Fran some of the rewards of self-evaluation.
> ("Break a leg" is the traditional hex-breaking
> toast offered to actors before an opening
> performance.)

Peyton, K.M.
FLAMBARDS   Gr.5+/$4.91L

Collins & World, 1968

> Role-playing in the traditional surroundings of
> the early 1900's. Flambards is an estate owned
> by Christina's uncle, and only when she decides
> to challenge the constraints of her society by
> eloping does she find both freedom and
> happiness.

Polland, Madeleine
STRANGER IN THE HILLS   Gr.3-7

Doubleday, 1968

> An escaped Russian sailor is aided and abetted
> by two independent-minded girls in Scotland.

Poole, Josephine
MOON EYES   Gr.5+/$4.95H

Little, Brown, 1967

> Kate's aunt is a conjurer of the supernatural,
> and the young girl is determined to save her
> brother and herself from the influences the
> aunt conjures up.

Portis, Charles
TRUE GRIT   Gr.4-7/$1.25P/$4.95H

Simon & Schuster, 1968

> Recently made into a film, this is the story of a
> spirited young girl who sets out to find her
> father's murderer.

Rankin, Louise
DAUGHTER OF   Gr.4-7/$.95P/$3.50H
THE MOUNTAINS

Viking, 1948

> A long and hazardous trail in search of her
> stolen dog leads Momo, a young girl, all the
> way to Calcutta from her home in Tibet.

Ransom, Arthur
SWALLOW AND AMAZONS   Gr.4-10

Lippincott, 1931

> Lots of adventure awaits a pair of brothers and
> sisters when they sail to a remote island. Each
> of them exhibits courage and resourcefulness.

Rich, Gibson
FIREGIRL   Gr.3+/$3.00P

Feminist Press, 1972

Brenda wants more than anything else to be a fire fighter. When her class visits the fire house, Brenda fills out an application form, writing down "Firegirl" where it says "Regular Fireman." Brenda gets her chance later on to prove her aptitude for fire fighting in a daring rescue.

Robinson, Jan M.
THE DECEMBER DOG   Gr.3-5/$3.75H

Lippincott, 1969

Kit finds freedom at last from the cruelty of a heartless master, and lives freely and happily by her own devices.

Robinson, Joan G.
CHARLEY   Gr.3-7/$5.95H

Coward, McCann & Geogheghan, 1970

Charley runs away because she thinks she is not wanted, and discovers that independence can be both a lonely and exciting experience.

WHEN MARNIE WAS THERE   Gr.3-7

Coward, McCann & Geoghegan, 1968

> When she meets the fascinating, if baffling,
> Marnie, Anna finds relief from the loneliness of
> her little seaside village.

Robinson, Mabel L.
STRONG WINGS   Gr.5-9

Random House, 1951

> Big responsibilities are thrust upon her when
> Connie finds herself and her siblings without
> money in their family's resort house in Maine.

Rock, Gail
THE HOUSE WITHOUT   Gr.3+/$3.95H
A CHRISTMAS TREE

Knopf, 1974

> A ten-year-old girl with an independent spirit
> and a sympathetic grandmother, tries, over her
> father's objections, to get a Christmas tree into
> the house.

Russ, Lavina
OVER THE HILLS   Gr.5-9/$5.50H
AND FAR AWAY

Harcourt Brace Jovanovich, 1968

> Peakie has two family examples she can follow
> as she grows up: her sister exemplifies the tra-

ditional "feminine" role, while her mother is deeply involved in the peace and labor movements of 1910.

Sachs, Marilyn
THE BEARS' HOUSE   Gr.4-7/$3.95H

Doubleday, 1971

Fran Ellen builds a wall between herself and others as a buffer against their discovering that she lives alone with her siblings. But even though she is anxious and has to suffer the taunts of her peers, she manages to retain her individuality and sense of pride.

PETER AND VERONICA   Gr.4-7/$4.50H

Doubleday, 1969

Veronica is the class bully who is befriended by Peter. He, in turn, has to defend himself against the taunting of this friends as well as the opposition of his family.

Scoppenttone, Sandra
SUZUKI BEANE   Gr.6+/$3.95H

Doubleday, 1961

The world through Suzuki's eyes as she tells about life with her mother, a sculptress, and her father, a poet.

Seredy, Kate
GOOD MASTER   Gr.3-7/$4.00H

Viking, 1935

> Rural Hungary in the "old days" is the setting
> for this story about a vibrant young girl from
> Budapest who lives on her uncle's farm for a
> year.

Sharp, Margery
MISS BIANCA   Gr.4+/$4.95H

Little, Brown, 1962

> This is the sequel to novelist Sharp's *The
> Rescuers.* It involves a commonsensical and
> brave white mouse with the Mouse Prisoners
> Aid Society.

Shemin, Margaretha
LITTLE RIDERS   Gr.2-6/$3.99L

Coward, McCann & Geoghegan

> While staying with her grandparents in Holland,
> an American girl helps preserve the symbols of
> their town's dignity and independence.

Snedeker, Caroline Dale
DOWNRIGHT DENCEY   Gr.4-7/$3.95H

Doubleday, 1927

> Dencey is not only "downright," but resource-
> ful as well, as she makes friends with an
> illiterate boy and helps him learn to read.

Snyder, Zilpha Keatley
THE CHANGELING   Gr.4-7/$.95P/$5.95H

Doubleday, 1927

> Weird Ivy Carson's friendship with their daughter, Martha, makes Martha's parents distinctly uncomfortable. Is Ivy really a changeling?

———————

THE EGYPT GAME   Gr.5-7/$1.95P/$6.95H

Atheneum, 1967

> The game devised by some children in the city becomes somewhat intense as they are menaced by a deranged person.

———————

THE HEADLESS CUPID   Gr.4-8/$1.95P/$4.95H

Atheneum, 1971

> As she is simply trying to entertain her sister and step-brother, Amanda accidentally conjures up a poltergeist. But, as a result, she finds herself feeling less antagonism to her new step-father and family.

Sobol, Donald
GRETA THE STRONG   Gr.4-6

Follett, 1970

> The traditional quest theme, only this time it

involves a courageous young woman who seeks King Arthur's sword, Excalibur.

Sorenson, Virginia
CURIOUS MISSIE   Gr.3-7/$5.50H

Harcourt Brace Jovanovich, 1953

Missie is far from a passive little girl as she goes to battle in her Alabama town to keep the bookmobile in circulation.

Southall, Ivan
ASH ROAD   Gr.5-9

St. Martin's Press, 1965

Two small town girls become heroines when their acts of courage during a fire help to keep the toll to a minimum.

WALK A MILE AND GET NOWHERE   Gr.5+

Bradbury Press, 1970

A lesson in the emptiness of macho as a thirteen-year-old puts his "manhood" to the test.

Speevack, Yetta
THE SPIDER PLANT   Gr.3-7/$3.25H

Atheneum, 1965

The story of how her resourcefulness helps

Carmen Santos and her brother adjust more readily to an alien atmosphere when they emigrate from Puerto Rico to New York City.

Spykman, E.C.
A LEMON AND A STAR   Gr.4-7/$5.95H

Harcourt Brace Jovanovich, 1955

All the children share the bizarre adventures in this turn-of-the-century tale.

Spyri, Johanna
HEIDI   Gr.3-7/$4.95H

Macmillan, 1880

The classic story of an orphan girl who lives in the Swiss mountains with her grandfather.

Sterling, Dorothy
MARY JANE   Gr.4-7/$4.95H

Doubleday, 1959

A story about integration through the eyes of Mary Jane, the first black student in her town's school.

Streatfield, Noel
BALLET SHOES   Gr.4-7/$5.39L

Random House, 1937

A childless, ageing bachelor, whose main interest is in collecting rocks, decides to adopt three orphan girls, each of whom ultimately blossoms into her own career.

THE MAGIC SUMMER   Gr.4-7

Random House, 1937

> Their environment in the rural Irish country-
> side is different from anything the Gareth
> children have ever known. What's more, all
> four children find themselves feeling freer and
> more independent than they had ever felt
> before.

THURSDAY'S CHILD   Gr.4-8/$4.50

Random House , 1971

> England at the turn of the century is the set-
> ting for the story of Margaret Thursday who
> runs away from an orphanage and fends for
> herself in a variety of challenging situations.
> She finds that the life of the theater suits both
> her temperament and her talent.

Swarthout, Glendon and Kathryn
THE BUTTON BOAT   Gr.4-7/$5.95H

Doubleday, 1969

> Depression-era survival of a ten-year-old and
> her younger brother involves a good deal of
> action and excitement.

Travers, Pamela L.
MARY POPPINS   Gr.4-7/$1.75P/$5.95H

Harcourt Brace Jovanovich, 1934

> The first of a classic series about an unusual
> and charming woman who literally floats out
> of the sky on an unbrella and into the life of
> the Banks family.

Udry, Janis May
SUNFLOWER GARDEN   Gr.2-5/$4.89L

Harvey House, 1969

> While gardening in idyllic peace, Pipsa, an
> Indian, saves her baby brother's life by killing a
> rattlesnake which is about to attack him.

Uhnak, Dorothy
THE WITNESS   Gr.4+/$4.95H

Simon & Schuster, 1968

> Written by an ex-cop, the story features a
> plainclothes woman who solves a case involving
> a murder in a street demonstration.

Van Ness Blair, Ruth
MARY'S MONSTER   Gr.2-6/$5.95H

Coward, McCann & Geoghegan, 1975

> Mary Ann Anning's discovery of Icthyosaurus
> bones created a great deal of excitement in the
> scientific community as well as in the town of
> Lyme Regis where she lived. In this lively fic-
> tionalized account, her discovery is laid against
> the background of England in the early 1800's.

Watson, Sally
MUKHTAR'S CHILDREN   Gr.3-7/$4.50H

Holt, Rhinehart & Winston, 1968

> A strongminded Arab girl persists in her pursuit
> of self-determination; she prevails upon her
> father to allow her many of her own choices
> for her education and future life.

MAGIC AT WYCHWOOD   Gr.4-7/$5.99H

Knopf, 1969

> An amusing satire of the chivalric code featur-
> ing Princess Elaine, an extroverted, fun-loving
> maiden, and her friends at Wychwood Castle.

White, E.B.
CHARLOTTE'S WEB   Gr.3-7/$1.25P/$4.95H

Harper & Row, 1952

> The story of Charlotte, the spider, who is able
> to save Wilbur the Pig's life because of her
> intelligence and self-possession. A classic.

Widerberg, Siv
(Translated by Verne Moberg)
I'M LIKE ME   Gr.5+/$1.95P

Feminist Press, 1973

> Amusing Swedish poems about boys and girls
> growing up.

Wiggin, Kate Douglas
REBECCA OF SUNNYBROOK FARM   Gr.4-7/$4.95H

Houghton Mifflin, 1903

> Before she grows into a woman Rebecca has a good deal to contend with when she goes to live with two cross and demanding aunts.

Wilder, Laura Ingalls
THE LITTLE HOUSE   Gr.3-7/$1.50P/$5.95H

Harper & Row, 1932

> This is the beginning of an eight-book series about a plucky family in pioneer days and their experiences in establishing a home in the wilderness.

Willard, Barbara
THE LARK AND THE LAUREL   Gr.5-7/$5.95H

Harcourt Brace Jovanovich, 1970

> Cecily Jolland is left to live with relatives when her father is forced to flee England upon the accession of Henry Tudor to the throne.

Photo courtesy UPI

THIRD GRADE THROUGH SEVENTH GRADE

NON-FICTION

Aldis, Dorothy
NOTHING IS IMPOSSIBLE: Gr.4-7/$5.50H
THE STORY OF BEATRIX POTTER

Atheneum, 1969

> Beatrix Potter became the world renowned
> author and illustrator of books for children
> despite the fact that she grew up in a family
> with an overbearing Victorian father.

Barth, Edna
I'M NOBODY, WHO ARE YOU?   Gr.4-6/$6.95H
THE STORY OF EMILY DICKINSON

Seabury, 1971

> This book includes some of her poems as well
> as a biography of a poet unique in American
> literature. Her great strength of character and
> enthusiasm for life more than compensated for
> her delicate health. Her work was not pub-
> lished until after her death.

Blackburn, Joyce
MARTHA BERRY   Gr.5-7/$4.50H

Lippincott, 1968

> The Berry Schools were dedicated to the
> improvement of education for Georgia's poor
> mountain children. Martha Berry, the founder,
> devoted her life to this cause.

Boylston, Helen
CLARA BARTON: Gr.3-7/$2.95H
FOUNDER OF THE RED CROSS

Random House, 1955

> Clara Barton set a precedent by becoming the
> first Red Cross nurse in an era when women led
> cloistered lives.

Brownmiller, Susan
SHIRLEY CHISHOLM: A BIOGRAPHY   Gr.4-8/$3.95H

Doubleday, 1970

> Shirley Chisholm was America's first black
> Congresswoman, and this is a story of her life.

Carruth, Ella Kaiser
SHE WANTED TO READ: Gr.3-7/$2.95H
THE STORY OF
MARY MACLEOD BETHUNE

Abingdon, 1966

> Mary MacCleod Bethune became president of a
> college after having begun her career as an
> illiterate cotton picker.

Crawford, Deborah
FOUR WOMEN IN A VIOLENT TIME   Gr.5-7/$4.50H

Crown, 1970

> The story of four women who emigrated to America at different times, but all of whom fought for religious freedom in the 17th century. Included are Mary Dyer, Anne Hutchinson, Lady Deborah Moody and Penelope Stout.

Dunnahoo, Terry
EMILY DUNNING: A PORTRAIT   Gr.4-6/$5.95H

Reilly and Lee, 1970

> Emily Dunning achieved the goal she desired, despite the antagonism she had to face. She became the first woman surgeon only after years of fighting against sex discrimination.

Faber, Doris
A COLONY LEADER   Gr.4-7/$3.40H
ANNE HUTCHINSON

Garrard, 1970

> Anne Hutchinson insists on thinking for herself; consequently, she has to face the combined wrath of both church and state in Massachusetts.

OH, LIZZIE! THE STORY OF   Gr.4-8/$5.95H
ELIZABETH CADY STANTON

Lothrop, Lee & Shepard, 1972

> Women's Liberation was not a popular issue in 1848, when Elizabeth Cady Stanton organized the first Women's Rights Convention.

Fleming, Alice
THE SENATOR FROM MAINE: Gr.3-8/$4.95H
MARGARET CHASE SMITH

Crowell, 1969

> The former Senator from Maine was the only woman who served both in the House and the Senate, and elected four times to the upper chamber.

Gersh, Harry
WOMEN WHO MADE AMERICA GREAT   Gr.4-7

Lippincott, 1962

> Their backgrounds and careers vary widely, and each made her own contribution to America's greatness.

Goldreich, Gloria and Esther
WHAT CAN SHE BE? A LAWYER   Gr.K-5/$4.75H

Lothrop, Lee & Shepard, 1973

> One of a series of books on various professions which young women looking for a career can

investigate. These volumes have pictures and text, this one dealing with a law career.

WHAT CAN SHE BE?   Gr.K-5/$4.75H
A VETERINARIAN

Lothrop, Lee & Shepard, 1973

Dr. Penny is a veterinarian; there are pictures of her on her daily rounds taking care of animals as well as text describing her work.

Hoyt, Mary Finch
AMERICAN WOMEN   Gr.5-10/$3.50H
OF THE SPACE AGE

Atheneum, 1966

The stories of women who participated in scientific experiments, computer technology, and research related to space programs.

Ingraham, Claire R. & Leonard W.
AN ALBUM OF WOMEN   Gr.4+/$4.33L
IN AMERICAN HISTORY

Franklin Watts, 1972

A description of the lives of American women, with an emphasis on individuals who have achieved some measure of fame. The first part of the book presents a historical picture beginning with Indian women and white and black women in Colonial America and up to both World Wars. The last part deals with women in the arts and sciences, sports and politics. Many illustrations, bibliography and index.

Juhl, Yuri
ELOQUENT CRUSADER: Gr.5-8/$3.50H
ERNESTINE ROSE

Messner, 1970

> The product of a Polish ghetto, Ernestine Rose
> joined the fight for women's rights alongside
> Susan B. Anthony.

Noble, Iris
EMMELINE AND HER DAUGHTERS: Gr.5-8/$3.50H
THE PANKHURST SUFFRAGETTES

Messner, 1971

> The suffragist movement in England was far
> more violent than in America, and among the
> best known political activists were the "Fight-
> ing Pankhursts," a family unique in its
> committment to the cause.

_____

ISRAEL'S GOLDA MEIR: Gr.4-8/$5.29L
PIONEER TO PRIME MINISTER

Messner, 1972

> A detailed treatment of the former Israeli
> Prime Minister.

Norris, Marianna
DONA FELISA   Gr.3-5

Dodd Mead & Co.

> The story of Dona Felisa, the former Mayor of
> San Juan, Puerto Rico.

Peterson, Helen Stone
JANE ADDAMS: Gr.3-5/$3.40H
PIONEER OF HULL HOUSE

Garrard, 1965

> Hull House, founded by Jane Addams, was a model for social settlements. She lived among the poor and had a sympathetic understanding of their problems and needs.

Phelan, Mary Kay
PROBING THE UNKNOWN: Gr.5-7/$4.95H
THE STORY OF DR. FLORENCE SABIN

Crowell, 1969

> At the turn of the century, when it was not common for women to pursue their own careers, Florence Sabin graduated from medical school and specialized in research. She also became pre-eminent as a public health officer and teacher.

Sabin, Francene
WOMEN WHO WIN   Gr.5+/$3.95H

Random House, 1975

> Fourteen women athletes are dealt with here. The biographical sketches not only discuss the athletic prowess of the champions, but also deal with the psychological and emotional obstacles which confronted them.

Seibert, Jerry
AMELIA EARHART: Gr.4-7/$2.20H
FIRST LADY OF THE AIR

Houghton Mifflin, 1960

> The story of one of America's most famous
> aviators from her childhood years up to her
> disappearance in the South Pacific, an event
> still shrouded in mystery.

Smith, Margaret Chase and Jeffers, Paul H.
GALLANT WOMEN   Gr.3-7/$4.72L

McGraw Hill, 1968

> Eleanor Roosevelt is one of the women dealt
> with in this study of twelve women and their
> varied careers.

Stevenson, Janet
WOMEN'S RIGHTS   Gr.5-7/$3.45L

Franklin Watts, 1972

> A calm and intelligent description of the back-
> ground to the granting of the vote to women.
> Illustrated with old photographs and woodcuts,
> and with a bibliography and index.

Wilkie, Katherine
MARIA MITCHELL: STARGAZER   Gr.2-5/$3.40H

Garrard, 1966

> As an accomplished astronomer, Maria Mitchell
> was an inspiration to many children who
> shared her fascination in the observation of
> heavenly bodies.

Wilson, Ellen
AMERICAN PAINTER IN PARIS:　　　Gr.4+/$4.95H
A LIFE OF MARY CASSATT

Farrar, Straus & Giroux, 1971

> One of the very few women painters who won
> the critical respect of her contemporaries, and
> whose work is still widely acclaimed.

Chapter Three

Seventh Grade through Twelfth Grade

From *Rally to the Death* by Douglas Rutherford

FICTION

Arundel, Honor
A FAMILY FAILING   Gr.6+/$4.95H

Nelson, 1972

> The reunification of Joanna's family would be
> an ideal ending to this story of family disinte-
> gration. But this is not a traditional ideal story,
> rather one in which the heroine learns the
> important lesson of self-reliance.

_____

THE LONGEST WEEKEND   Gr.7+/$4.95H

Nelson, 1970

> A very modern story about a pregnant young
> girl who defers marriage to her child's father
> because he is not yet mature enough to be a
> responsible husband and family man.

Bagnold, Enid
NATIONAL VELVET   Gr.6-9/$6.95H

Morrow, 1949

> The scene is the great Grand National and the

exciting story of a young girl whose horse is entered in the race.

Balderson, Margaret
WHEN JAYS FLY TO BARBMO   Gr.7-10/$4.91L

Collins & World, 1969

During the second World War the Germans occupied a Norwegian island. One of the inhabitants, fourteen year old Ingeborg, looks after her ailing aunt with a wood troll named Per for company, as friends and relatives are taken to prison or to their deaths.

Beyer, Audrey White
KATHERINE LESLIE   Gr.7-10

Knopf, 1963

18th century London is the scene where Katherine Leslie is unjustly accused of a crime and sentenced to a long prison term. How she escapes makes an adventurous tale.

Bolton, Carole
NEVER JAM TODAY   Gr.5-9/$.95P/$5.25H

Atheneum, 1973

For simply picketing the White House in 1917, a group of suffragists are given a choice of a fine or a jail sentence. Maddy, a seventeen-year-old activist for women's rights, chooses to go to jail. She also works her way through college and continues her women's rights activism.

Burt, Olive
WIND BEFORE THE DAWN   Gr.7-10

Day, 1964

> The story of the Mormons' difficult journey to
> the West is told through the personal experi-
> ences of a teen-aged heroine.

Cleaver, Vera & Bill
THE WHYS AND WHEREFORES   Gr.7+/$5.95H
OF LITTABELLE LEE

Atheneum, 1973

> Littabelle Lee is a tough-minded young woman
> of sixteen who is left alone with her grand-
> parents to cope with the mysteries and irration-
> alities of human existence. She learns a great
> deal. The book abounds with colorfully-named
> characters: Maw Maw and Paw Paw, Aunt
> Sorrow, Winston Splitstone, Judge Marriage.

Colman, Hila
CLAUDIA, WHERE ARE YOU?   Gr.7-10/$5.11L

Morrow, 1969

> Claudia leaves high school in her senior year
> and goes to Greenwich Village in New York to
> live a new and independent life.

DAUGHTER OF DISCONTENT   Gr.7+/$5.95H

Morrow, 1971

> A daughter must come to grips with her own

mixed, if not hostile, feelings about her over-bearing father as well as her attitudes towards men in general.

Corcoran, Barbara
DON'T SLAM THE DOOR   Gr.5-9/$5.95H
WHEN YOU GO

Atheneum, 1972

The book is full of young people trying to "get their heads together." The problem is compounded by their realization of the indifference apparently greeting their departure from home.

SAM   Gr.5-9/$.95P/$4.25H

Atheneum, 1967

Sam is the daughter of a misanthropic father who moves the family to a nearby island. Sam has to go through an arduous process of undoing some of her preconceived notions before she comes to grips with "civilized" life.

Crane, Caroline
DON'T LOOK AT ME THAT WAY   Gr.7-10/$5.39L

Random House, 1970

How an eighteen-year-old Puerto Rican girl copes with the exigencies of survival in New York's hectic, noisy life.

Crary, Margaret
SUZETTE LA FLESCHE: Gr.7-12/$5.95H
VOICE OF THE OMAHA INDIANS

Hawthorn, 1973

> Suzette La Flesche received her education off the reservation, like a white woman. She devoted many years of her life to drawing the public's attention to the Indians' cause. Fictionalized additions to the story are included along with photographs.

Crawford, Deborah
SOMEBODY WILL MISS ME   Gr.7+/$4.95H

Crown, 1971

> Change is the keynote of this Depression-era story about Abby, a twelve-year-old whose outlook is more than a little different from the grandparents who raised her.

de Jong, Dola
BETWEEN HOME AND HORIZON   Gr.7+/$4.59L

Knopf, 1962

> Two lifestyles are adopted by twin girls: one becomes a professional musician, the other a wife and mother.

Duncombe, Frances Riker
CASSIE'S VILLAGE   Gr.7-10/$5.25H

Lothrop, Lee & Shepard, 1965

> A young girl's resourcefulness is responsible for saving a village which could be flooded by the construction of a dam.

Engdahl, Sylvia L.
ENCHANTRESS FROM   Gr.7-10/$.95P/$6.50H
THE STARS

Atheneum, 1970

> A unique fantasy with meaningful allegory:
> Elana, a young anthropologist from a civiliza-
> tion superior to ours, has to prove herself
> through exploration of a planet whose culture
> is roughly comparable to that which existed in
> the Middle Ages.

THE FAR SIDE OF EVIL   Gr.5+/$.95P/$6.50H

Atheneum, 1971

> Another story which depicts Elana as a heroic
> figure. This time she saves a planet from
> destroying itself. Her coolness and determina-
> tion are doubly admirable since she also has to
> cope with a male associate on her team who
> goes to pieces under the pressure of
> circumstances.

Engelbrecht, P.A.
UNDER THE HAYSTACK   Gr.6+/$4.95H

Nelson, 1973

> Thirteen-year-old Sandy becomes head of the
> household when her mother deserts her and her
> two sisters.

Fisher, Aileen and Rabe, Olive
WE DICKINSONS   Gr.7-10/$4.50H

Atheneum, 1965

> Emily Dickinson's brother, Austin, is depicted as telling the family's story. A fictionalized account, including quotations from the poems.

Fox, Paula
BLOWFISH LIVE IN THE SEA   Gr.6-8/$.75P/$5.95H

Bradbury Press, 1970

> Ben, nineteen, is thirteen-year-old Carrie's half-brother, both of whom live with their mother and Carrie's father, a doctor in New York. Ben is moody and rebellious, and a crisis occurs when Ben's father, after a twelve-year silence, writes to Ben to meet him in Boston. Ben and Carrie go to Boston together and enter a strange and rather frightening world. Ben's father offers him a way to resolve his troubled adolescence; Carrie is supportive, yet retains her individuality.

———————

THE STONE-FACED BOY   Gr.6+/$4.95H

Bradbury Press, 1968

> Gus, the third of five children, lives in an old house in the country with his parents and brothers and sisters. He is close to his younger sister Serena, but he finds it hard to cope with the others, and he is afraid of some rooms in the house. Despite his many fears, he saves an old dog that Serena loves, and, in a way, resolves some of his doubts about himself.

Fritzhand, James
LIFE IS A LONELY PLACE   Gr.7+/$5.95H

M. Evans, 1975

> Tink, who is fifteen years old, and lives in
> Maine, runs into difficulty with his over-
> bearing, demanding father, especially when the
> boy makes friends with a young writer from
> New York and begins to date a local girl with a
> doubtful reputation. Tink, who has always
> been an outsider, even in his own family, must
> come to some kind of adjustment with himself
> and with the people around him.

Gates, Doris
BLUE WILLOW   Gr.6-8/$.95P

Viking, 1940

> Janey Larkins, the daughter of immigrants,
> finally finds the permanent home she longs for.

George, Jean Craighead
JULIE OF THE WOLVES   Gr.7+/$6.95L

Harper & Row, 1972

> The wild Alaskan landscape is the setting for
> this story about an Eskimo girl who inadvert-
> ently wanders into wolf territory, but who also
> discovers the central importance of being self-
> reliant. Newbery Medal Winner.

Harris, Christie
CONFESSIONS OF A TOE-HANGER   Gr.6-10/$4.50H

Atheneum, 1967

> In a good-humored retrospective of her life, Feeny tells about her battle against conformity.

Hart, Carolyn
RENDEZVOUS IN VERA CRUZ   Gr.7-10/$4.95H

M. Evans, 1970

> In Mexico, Lin Prescott is innocently caught in a web of political intrigue.

Jensen, Ann
THE TIME OF ROSIE   Gr.7+/$3.25H

Steck-Vaughn, 1967

> Rosie is the name of the orphaned pig Anita Ogden's mother finally lets her adopt. Her mother runs the ranch and supervises all the help by herself. Anita's relationship to her and her experiences with Rosie make for warmth and humor.

Johnson, Annabel and Edgar
A PECULIAR MAGIC   Gr.7-10/$3.25H

Houghton Mifflin, 1965

> Cindy, while trying to locate her mother, joins a group of traveling actors in the Wild West.

Jordan, Hope Dahle
HAUNTED SUMMER   Gr.7-10/$4.95H

Lothrop, Lee & Shepard, 1967

> Rilla Marsten becomes a hit-and-run driver
> after she accidentally knocks down a bicycle
> rider, but ultimately she must face up to her
> act of cowardice.

Kamm, Josephine
THE STORY OF FANNY BURNEY   Gr.6-10

Hawthorn, 1967

> In the 18th century, Fanny Burney was one of
> England's most popular novelists. This is a fic-
> tionalized account of her life.

Klein, Norma
IT'S NOT WHAT YOU EXPECT   Gr.7+/$4.95H

Pantheon, 1973

> Parental separation and a friend's abortion are
> two of the traumas which confront twin broth-
> ers and their sister. Carla, a fourteen-year-old,
> wrestles with the complications involved in her
> parents' decision to have a trial separation, and
> her own insecurities and conflicting emotions.

MOM, THE WOLFMAN AND ME   Gr.5-9/$4.95H

Pantheon, 1972

> Brett's name for her mother's new friend is

"The Wolfman," someone she considers an interloper in her and her mother's tranquil life. How Brett fights against the growing inevitability of her mother's marriage makes a lively, amusing and often moving story.

Madden, Betsy
THE ALL-AMERICAN COEDS   Gr.7+/$4.25H

Criterion, 1971

The prohibition of co-ed basketball competition is broken down by a girls' team in a black school.

Masefield, Judith
SHEPHERDESS OF FRANCE: Gr.5-9
REMEMBRANCES OF JEANNE D'ARC

Coward, McCann & Geoheghan, 1969

Told in the first person, this fictionalized version of Jeanne D'Arc's life takes her from her childhood years to her martyrdom.

Nevin, Evelyn C.
THE EXTRAORDINARY   Gr.6-12/$.95P/$4.88L
ADVENTURES OF
CHEE-CHEE MC NERNEY

Four Winds, 1971

Chee-Chee, accompanied by a trio of strange companions, encounters adventure on her trip to the Yukon. Thanks to her sense of humor, she manages very well.

Newell, Hope
A CAP FOR MARY ELLIS   Gr.7-10/$4.79L

Harper & Row, 1952

>The story of a young black girl whose ambition
>to be a nurse leads her to become one of the
>first black students to enroll in an all white
>school.

Peyton, K.M.
MAPLIN BIRD   Gr.7-10

Collins & World, 1965

>An "escape" story taking place in the 1880's.
>An orphaned brother and sister leave the strin-
>gent protection of their aunt and uncle to build
>a life of their own.

Rabe, Berneice
NAOMI   Gr.7+/$6.95H

Nelson, 1975

>Naomi, a farm girl in Missouri in the late
>1930's, lives in a repressive atmosphere, filled
>with ignorance and superstition. When a for-
>tune-teller tells her she will die before her 14th
>birthday, Naomi must face up to attitudes of
>her family, especially her mother, and decide
>what they really mean to her. She rejects the
>idea of marriage at the age of fourteen or
>fifteen, the custom in her area, and decides
>instead to become a doctor.

Randall, Florence Engel
THE ALMOST YEAR   Gr.6-8/$5.95H

Atheneum, 1971

> Tensions and youthful emotionalism erupt, unleashing a poltergeist in the home of a white suburban family among whose residents is a black teen-age girl from the city.

Robinson, Mabel L.
BRIGHT ISLAND   Gr.7-9/$5.69L

Random House, 1937

> The freedom of her island life must come to an end for Curtis who has to leave home to go to school.

Rutherford, Douglas
RALLY TO THE DEATH   Gr.6-8/$5.95H

Bradbury Press, 1974

> Eighteen-year-old Kate is driving in the 2,300 mile Rally of the Forests in this English novel. The *Daily Post* is sponsoring her, and a nasty group called the Rough Justice Commandos is trying to stop her because they dislike the *Post*. Much of the action in the story centers on Kate's young male friends, but she is able to drive very skillfully and is able to hold her own against the other drivers who respect her ability.

Sargent, Shirley
RANGER IN SKIRTS   Gr.7-10

Abingdon, 1966

> As a student of the natural sciences, a young
> woman uses and sharpens her knowledge while
> working as a ranger in Yosemite National Park.

Speare, Elizabeth George
THE WITCH OF BLACKBIRD POND   Gr.7-10/$4.95H

Houghton Mifflin, 1958

> Kit, born in Barbados, rebuffs Puritan pressures
> to conform in a New England town, and earns
> the title of witch.

Stolz, Mary
BY THE HIGHWAY HOME   Gr.7+/$4.95H

Harper & Row, 1971

> Not only has her brother been killed in the
> Vietnam War, but thirteen-year-old Cathy's
> father has lost his job. In this atmosphere of
> tension, her mother and father and her siblings
> must come to terms with the inexplicable
> tragedy which has been inflicted upon them.

Swinburne, Laurence
DETLI   Gr.7-10/$5.00H

Bobbs-Merrill, 1970

> A strong-minded immigrant living in a mining
> town in Pennsylvania is convinced she bears the
> spirit of a reincarnated queen.

Winthrop, Elizabeth
A LITTLE DEMONSTRATION   Gr.7+/$5.95H
OF AFFECTION

Harper & Row, 1975

John, Jenny and Charley are three children in a
family where there is good will, but little open
affection. John and Jenny spend much time
together and Charley is an intruder. One summer when John goes away, Jenny and Charley
become very close, so close that when Charley
becomes attracted to her friend Lucy, Jenny is
jealous and frightened by her feelings. It is a
summer when the whole family learns about
open demonstration of affection.

Wojciechowska, Maia
DON'T PLAY DEAD   Gr.7+/$4.43L
BEFORE YOU HAVE TO

Harper & Row, 1970

A five-year-old is "adopted" by a sympathetic
teenage boy.

Zindel, Paul
THE PIGMAN   Gr.7-10/$4.95H

Harper & Row, 1968

In their growing friendship with Mr. Pignati, an
elderly and somewhat eccentric man, two teen-
agers, a boy and a girl, unwittingly exploit him.

Photo courtesy UPI

Margaret Sanger

SEVENTH GRADE THROUGH TWELFTH GRADE

NON-FICTION

Adams, Jean and Kimball, Margaret
HEROINES OF THE SKY   Gr.5-9/$18.25H

Books for Libraries, 1942

> Studies of Amelia Earhart and nine other
> women flyers in the early days of aviation.

Archer, Jules
THE UNPOPULAR ONES   Gr.7-10/$3.95H

Crowell-Collier, 1968

> A biography of fifteen women who were ahead
> of their time in agitating for social change.
> Among these are Amelia Jenks Bloomer, jour-
> nalist Ann Royall and birth control advocate
> Margaret Sanger.

Auriol, Jacqueline
I LIVE TO FLY   Gr.7+/$5.95H

Dutton, 1970

> Her return to the profession is described by the
> world's only woman test pilot.

Bernard, Jacqueline
JOURNEY TOWARDS FREEDOM: Gr.5-9
THE STORY OF SOJOURNER TRUTH

Grossett & Dunlap, 1967

>This is the story of former slave Sojourner
>Truth who travelled the lecture circuit after the
>Civil War to speak out on social issues affecting
>women, prisoners and working people.

Bigland, Eileen
QUEEN ELIZABETH I   Gr.7-10/$3.50H

Criterion, 1965

>One of the most dynamic monarchs in history,
>Elizabeth I was a strong and complicated
>woman. This vivid biography has caught her
>unique spirit.

Block, Irwin
NEIGHBOR TO THE WORLD: Gr.6-9/$4.95H
THE STORY OF LILLIAN WALD

Crowell, 1969

>Lillian Wald was a pioneer in securing the
>establishment of many social facilities we now
>take for granted: playgrounds, school health
>programs, settlement houses.

Bonham, Barbara
WILLA CATHER   Gr.6-10/$4.25H

Chilton, 1970

>Willa Cather became one of America's most

respected novelists; she began her career as a teacher and editor.

Borer, Mary Cathcart
WOMEN WHO MADE HISTORY   Gr.7-10

Warne, 1963

Sketches of a number of noteworthy women from the eighteenth to the twentieth centuries.

Brown, Marion Marsh and Crone, Ruth
WILLA CATHER   Gr.7+/$4.50H

Scribner, 1970

A second well-rounded and thoughtful biography of one of America's best known novelists who began her professional career as a journalist and teacher.

———————

SILENT STORM   Gr.7-10/$4.95H

Abingdon, 1963

The story of Anne Sullivan Macy, the woman who taught deaf and blind Helen Keller how to talk; an interesting, balanced account.

Buckmaster, Henrietta
WOMEN WHO SHAPED HISTORY   Gr.7-11/$4.95H

Crowell-Collier, 1966

Biographical sketches of a handful of 19th

century Americans who attempted to free both men and women from the social strictures which limited them.

Carlson, Dale
GIRLS ARE EQUAL TOO   Gr.6+/$6.95H

Atheneum, 1975

In this book for teenage girls, they are told what they can expect from life and what they ought to expect as mature women. This is a primer on the Woman's Movement: how it evolved, how women became what they are, and, finally, how women can assert greater control over their destinies. Amusing illustrations.

Chisholm, Shirley
UNBOUGHT AND UNBOSSED   Gr.9+/$5.95H

Houghton Mifflin, 1970

The Shirley Chisholm story as told by herself, and how she has felt more discriminated against as a woman than as a black person.

Cintron, Conchita
MEMOIRS OF A BULLFIGHTER   Gr.7-11

Holt, Rinehart & Winston

Her own story of the discrimination she has suffered as the only woman torero in the world.

Conn, Frances G.
IDA TARBELL, MUCKRAKER $4.95H

Nelson, 1972

> Muckraking, a good old American journalistic tradition, was begun by Ida Tarbell in the 1900's.

Coolidge, Olivia
WOMEN'S RIGHTS: THE SUFFRAGE   Gr.7-10/$6.95
MOVEMENT IN AMERICA 1848-1920

Dutton, 1966

> A solid history of the movement, including photographs.

DeGering, Etta
WILDERNESS WIFE: THE STORY   Gr.7-10/$3.95H
OF REBECCA BRYAN BOONE

McKay, 1966

> How Daniel Boone's wife shared the trials and tribulations of pioneering along with her husband.

DeMille, Agnes
TO A YOUNG DANCER   Gr. 7-10/$5.95H

Little, Brown, 1962

> The pains and the satisfactions of the life of dance, as told by one of the world's best known practitioners of the art form.

Dribben, Judith Strick
A GIRL CALLED JUDITH STRICK   Gr.10+/$7.95H

Cowles, 1970

>   The story of a young Jewish girl who became a
>   soldier in the Israeli army after having lived
>   through imprisonment in a Nazi concentration
>   camp.

Faber, Doris
PETTICOAT POLITICS: HOW   Gr.7-10/$4.59H
AMERICAN WOMEN WON
THE RIGHT TO VOTE

Lothrop, Lee & Shepard, 1967

>   How women in America finally won their
>   seemingly endless battle for the franchise.

Fleming, Alice
DOCTORS IN PETTICOATS   Gr.7-10

Lippincott, 1964

>   How ten women fought, and won, to have
>   careers in medicine, and how some of them
>   contributed to medical advances.

GREAT WOMEN TEACHERS   Gr.7-10

Lippincott, 1965

>   The stories of ten women educators and their
>   careers, spanning more than one hundred years.

Garnett, Emmeline
MADAM PRIME MINISTER: THE   Gr.7-10/$4.50H
STORY OF INDIRA GANDHI

Farrar, Straus & Giroux, 1967

> Written in a happier time for the Prime Minister, the story of the first woman to achieve that office. The book also provides some insight into India's independence movement.

Gibson, Althea and Curtis, Richard
SO MUCH TO LIVE FOR   Gr.7-10/$4.29L

Putnam, 1968

> When Althea Gibson retired from tennis in 1958, she wrote this story about her life as a sportswoman and as a person.

Greenfield, Howard
GERTRUDE STEIN: A BIOGRAPHY   Gr.7+/$5.95H

Crown, 1973

> Gertrude Stein lived in Paris from the early 1900's. She was in the forefront of the new wave of literature as well as an early patron of the Impressionists.

Grey, Elizabeth
FRIEND WITHIN THE GATES: Gr.7-10/$3.95H
THE STORY OF EDITH CAVELL

Houghton Mifflin, 1961

> Edith Cavell was an English nurse who estab-

lished a para-nursing service in Belgium, and was also a leader of the resistance movement in that country during the first World War.

Guthrie, Anne
MADAME AMBASSADOR   Gr.7-10/$4.95H

Harcourt Brace Jovanovich, 1962

Vijaya Lakshmi Pandit, Nehru's sister, was the woman who became president of the U.N. General Assembly in its 8th term; she was also an activist in India's campaign for independence.

Harmelink, Barbara
FLORENCE NIGHTINGALE: FOUNDER   Gr.7+/$4.33L
OF MODERN NURSING

Franklin Watts, 1969

Florence Nightingale was from a "good" family, and the idea of her working upset them considerably. She was not only a good nurse, but a first rate administrator who revolutionized hospital care.

Hughes, Langston
FAMOUS
AMERICAN NEGROES   Gr.7-9/$1.75P/$3.95H

Dodd Mead & Co., 1954

One of America's best known poets, Langston Hughes, writes about a number of black women who fought for human rights and justice.

Hume, Ruth Fox
GREAT WOMEN OF MEDICINE   Gr.6-10/$5.69L

Random House, 1964

> Biographies of several American women pioneers in the field of medicine.

Johnson, Eleanor Noyes
MRS. PERLEY'S PEOPLE   Gr.6-9/$4.95L

Westminster, 1970

> Helen Perley's scientific curiosity began at an early age. Her observations about animals are widely known and respected, and are dealt with in this biography.

Jones, Dorothy Holder and Sargent, Ruth Sexton
ABBIE BURGESS: Gr.7-10/$4.95H
LIGHTHOUSE HEROINE

Funk & Wagnalls, 1969

> In 1857 at Mantinicus Rock in Maine, the weather was violent and destructive, and fourteen-year-old Abbie Burgess acted with great courage.

Klein, Mina C. and H. Arthur
KATHE KOLLWITZ: LIFE IN ART   Gr.7+/$11.95H

Holt, Rinehart & Winston, 1972

> A first rate biography of one of the most dynamic artists of the 20th century. Kathe

Kollwitz's subjects reflect her deep concern for human beings, and she was a conscious feminist.

Komisar, Lucy
THE NEW FEMINISM   Gr.6-12/$6.88L

Franklin Watts, 1971

Some straight talk about feminism from a leading activist in the Woman's Movement. She discusses feminism in a historical perspective as well as its resurgence in the last decade and how it is likely to affect the individual now and in the future.

Lader, Lawrence and Meltzer, Milton
MARGARET SANGER: PIONEER   Gr.7-10/$4.95H
OF BIRTH CONTROL

Crowell, 1969

A study of the determined, single-minded woman in her life-long efforts to ease restrictive abortion laws, and to establish the first clinic devoted to birth control.

Lavine, Sigmund
EVANGELINE BOOTH: Gr.7-10/$4.95H
DAUGHTER OF SALVATION

Dodd Mead & Co., 1970

The story of how the vast, international Salvation Army was built under the efficient administrative direction of Evangeline Booth.

Leighton, Margaret
CLEOPATRA: SISTER   Gr.7-10/$3.95H
OF THE MOON

Farrar, Straus & Giroux, 1969

> In this interesting biographical critique, Cleopatra is seen not only in her relationships with Caesar and Antony, but also as a monarch and diplomat.

Longsworth, Polly
I, CHARLOTTE FORTEN,   Gr.7-10/$4.95H
BLACK AND FREE

Crowell, 1970

> Charlotte Forten, as a fervent abolitionist, spent her life helping other blacks to become free.

McHugh, Mary
LAW AND THE NEW WOMAN   Gr.7+/$5.90H

Franklin Watts, 1975

> This is the first of a forthcoming series of guides to the professions for women. This volume is for young women who may want to become lawyers or paralegals. It contains chapters, among others, on law schools, corporate, private and public service law practices as well as a chapter on combining a family and a career. A list of law schools approved by the ABA is also included.

Meltzer, Milton
TONGUE OF FLAME: THE LIFE   Gr.7-10/$4.95H
OF LYDIA MARIA CHILD

Crowell, 1965

> Lydia Maria Child wrote on a number of political topics; among her works was the first book in the United States on abolitionism.

Merriam, Eve
INDEPENDENT VOICES   Gr.10+/$4.25H

Atheneum, 1968

> Verse biographies of seven independent-spirited people, four men and three women.

Meyer, Edith Patterson
FIRST LADY OF THE RENAISSANCE: Gr.6+
A BIOGRAPHY OF ISABELLA D'ESTE

Little, Brown, 1970

> Isabella D'Este was married to a career soldier who was frequently away from home. As a result, she became an independent-thinking woman who was able to use her wit and resourcefulness to influence monarchs and stimulate artists.

Miller, Helen
WOMAN DOCTOR OF THE WEST   Gr.7-10

Messner, 1960

> The story of a woman physician who had to cope with a good deal of harassment on her way to becoming a surgeon.

Moore, Carman
SOMEBODY'S ANGEL CHILD: Gr.7-10/$4.95H
THE STORY OF BESSIE SMITH

Crowell, 1969

> Bessie Smith led a triumphant, but, in the end,
> a tragic life. She was the greatest blues singer of
> all time, and much of the sadness she sang
> about was her own personal story of the blues.

Morris, Terry
SHALOM, GOLDA   Gr.5-10/$6.95H

Hawthorn, 1971

> The story of Golda Meir, former Prime Minister
> of Israel, from her early years in an obscure
> Russian town to her ultimate political victory.

Nathan, Dorothy
WOMEN OF COURAGE   Gr.7-10/$.75P/$2.95H

Random House, 1964

> Biographies of five American women pre-
> eminent in their respective fields:
> anthropologist Margaret Mead, pilot Amelia
> Earhart, social worker Jane Addams, women's
> rights pioneer Susan B. Anthony, and Mary
> MacLeod Bethune, civil rights leader.

Noble, Iris
NELLIE BLY, FIRST WOMAN REPORTER   Gr.6-9

Messner, 1956

> The first woman in any male dominated field

must not only be good at what she does, but must also be prepared to cope with discrimination. As the first woman reporter, Nellie Bly always had to be on her guard.

Oakley, Mary Ann B.
ELIZABETH CADY STANTON   Gr.9+/$2.75P

Feminist Press, 1973

Two women are considered keystones of the feminist movement in America: Susan B. Anthony and, her associate, Elizabeth Cady Stanton. This biography covers the essentials of her career as a major organizer of the Seneca Falls Convention, her lecturing on religion and marriage as well as women's suffrage, and that she was the mother of seven children.

Petry, Ann
HARRIET TUBMAN: CONDUCTOR   Gr.7-10/$4.95H
ON THE UNDERGROUND RAILROAD

Crowell, 1955

Harriet Tubman was herself an escaped slave. For ten years before the outbreak of the Civil War she retraced her steps many times in order to lead other slaves to freedom.

Reiss, Johanna
THE UPSTAIRS ROOM   Gr.5-8/$4.50H

Crowell, 1972

For two years during the second World War, a Dutch family hid two Jewish girls in a room in their House. An interesting insight into how young people manage to function well even in such abnormal circumstances.

Ross, Pat
YOUNG AND FEMALE   Gr.6+/$4.95H

Random House, 1972

> A collection of sketches, extracted from their autobiographical works, by eight American women who talk about the turning point in their lives. They include Margaret Sanger, Althea Gibson, Margaret Bourke-White, Shirley MacLaine, Dorothy Dan and Emily Hahn.

Scott, John A. & Meltzer, Milton
FANNY KEMBLE'S AMERICA   Gr.5-9/$4.95H

Crowell, 1973

> Fanny Kemble emigrated to America before the outbreak of the Civil War. Although best known then as an actress, she earned an equally high reputation as a woman of letters.

Shafter, Toby
EDNA ST. VINCENT MILLAY   Gr.7+/$3.34L

Messner, 1959

> The life story of a unique American poet.

Shulman, Alix
TO THE BARRICADES   Gr.7-10/$4.95H
THE ANARCHIST LIFE
OF EMMA GOLDMAN

Crowell, 1971

> Emma Goldman, who died in 1940, was concerned in her lifetime with social issues that

still concern us: the anonymity of bureaucracy, women's rights, peace.

Sterling, Dorothy
FREEDOM TRAIN: THE   Gr.7-10/$3.95H
STORY OF HARRIET TUBMAN

Doubleday, 1954

> Another study of Harriet Tubman who was responsible for smuggling more than three hundred slaves out of the South.

LUCRETIA MOTT   Gr.7+

Doubleday, 1964

> Lucretia Mott helped organize the first Women's Rights Congress as well as founded the Female Anti-Slavery Society.

Sterling, Philip
SEA AND EARTH: THE   Gr.7-10/$4.95H
LIFE OF RACHEL CARSON

Crowell, 1970

> When *The Silent Spring* was first published in the early 1960's, Rachel Carson's warnings about the danger of insecticides were scoffed at by many critics. But today her observations have been corroborated: this is the story of her life and of the impact of her books.

Stiller, Richard
QUEEN OF POPULISTS: Gr.7-10/$4.95H
THE STORY OF
MARY ELIZABETH LEASE

Crowell, 1970

> In the 1890's, Mary Elizabeth Lease was leader
> of the Populist Party and thus became the first
> woman political figure of national significance.

Stoddard, Hope
FAMOUS AMERICAN WOMEN   Gr.7-11/$7.50H

Crowell, 1970

> More than forty biographical accounts of
> women from a variety of backgrounds who
> were dedicated to varied causes and careers,
> from the 18th to the 20th centuries.

Sutton, Margaret
PALACE WAGON FAMILY: A TRUE   Gr.6+/$5.69H
STORY OF THE DONNER PARTY

Knopf, 1957

> The true-to-life account of a hazardous wagon
> trip taken by the Donner Party in 1846.

Taylor, Kathryn
GENERATIONS OF DENIAL   Gr.7+/$1.75P

Times Change Press, 1971

> Short biographical sketches of seventy-five
> women in history.

Thurman, Judith
I BECAME ALONE   Gr.7+/$6.25H

Atheneum, 1975

>Five women poets from antiquity to the 19th
>century are dealt with here: Sapho, Louise
>Labe, Anne Bradstreet, Juana Ines de la Cruz
>and Emily Dickinson. Each biographical sketch
>also includes a selection of the author's poems.

Vipont, Elfrida
TOWARDS A HIGH ATTIC: THE   Gr.6+/$4.59L
EARLY LIFE OF GEORGE ELIOT

Holt, Rinehart, Winston, 1971

>George Eliot became one of England's leading
>Victorian novelists. As a young woman she was
>self-conscious about her plainness, but she
>learned to assess her own true value and to
>mine her considerable talent.

Werstein, Irving
LABOR'S DEFIANT LADY: Gr.7-10/$4.95H
THE STORY OF MOTHER JONES

Crowell, 1969

>As a staunch opponent of child labor, Mother
>Jones was a tough-minded labor organizer who
>also fought for the eight hour day.

Wise, Winifred
FANNY KEMBLE: ACTRESS,   Gr.7-10/$4.19L
AUTHOR, ABOLITIONIST

Putnam, 1966

> Her own rights, as well as the rights of slaves,
> were of concern to Fanny Kemble who was
> best known as an actress.

Wojciechowska, Maia
TILL THE BREAK OF DAY   Gr.7+/$5.50H

Harcourt Brace Jovanovich, 1972

> An autobiographical account of her life up to
> the time she came to America in 1945. Her
> recollections, because they are complex and
> told in retrospect, are at once joyful and pain-
> ful for her and she manages to communicate
> this to the reader.

Chapter Four

All Ages

Photo courtesy United Nations

Eleanor Roosevelt

ALL AGES

FICTION
and
NON-FICTION

Blume, Judy
IT'S NOT THE END OF THE WORLD $5.95H

Bradbury Press, 1972

> Eleven-year-old Karen tells this story, in the first person, of her parents' separation, and of how she and her big brother and little sister come to grips with the idea that a divorce is inevitable. A story of a child's adjustment to an adult world told with a good deal of humor and shrewd insight.

Baum, Frank L.
THE WIZARD OF OZ   Various Editions

Random House, 1969

> The classic tale of Dorothy who helps her new-found friends on their respective quests for missing parts and emotions.

Carroll, Lewis
ALICE'S ADVENTURES IN WONDERLAND $.95P
and THROUGH THE LOOKING GLASS

Macmillan, 1865, 1923, 1956, 1963
(A number of other editions)

> The classic tale of Alice's bizarre adventures on the other side of reality.

Frank, Anne
THE DIARY OF A YOUNG GIRL $.95P

Franklin Watts, Doubleday and other editions

This startling diary of a young Jewish girl who
was put to death in Belsen concentration camp
in 1945 has become a classic. While her death is
the most dramatic truth about Anne Frank, it
is her perception of life that makes this book
must reading.

Hazer, Nancy
GROWNUPS CRY, TOO $1.75P

Lollipop Power, 1973

Tears are — or should be — as natural to men as
to women, to grownups as to children. Tears
honestly express our real feelings, sometimes
out of happiness, sometimes sadness.

Kerr, M.E.
IS THAT YOU, MISS BLUE? $6.50H

Harper & Row, 1975

Flanders Brown goes to a boarding school in
Virginia after her mother leaves her father,
apparently for a man several years younger
than she. At school Flanders meets some odd
people, both students and faculty, the most
striking of the latter being Miss Blue, who talks
to Jesus. Everyone has some kind of problem
and tries to cope with it in his or her own way,
and Flanders learns something about human
nature and about her own parents.

LOVE IS A MISSING PERSON $5.95H

Harper & Row, 1975

> Suzy Slade, fifteen-year-old, lives with her mother. Her seventeen-year-old sister, Chicago, lives with their millionaire father. When Chicago comes to stay with Suzy and her mother, because of their father's new marriage, Suzy becomes aware of a tangle of other people's emotions. Chicago tries to cause a kind of revolution in the town and stirs up a lot of feeling, most of it bad. In the end, Suzy finds no answers but learns a lot about people.

Raynor, Dorka
THIS IS MY FATHER AND ME $4.25H

Albert Whitman, 1973

> Touching and arresting photographs of fathers and their children in more than twenty countries and the U.S.A.

Seed, Suzanne
SATURDAY'S CHILD $4.95P

J. Philip O'Hara, 1973

> A straightforward insight into thirty-six jobs performed by women. Jobs include architect, carpenter, cab driver, bank vice-president. Each woman talks about her job, how she chose it and what about it interests her. Each entry is accompanied by a photograph of the subject.

INDEX — AUTHORS

INDEX — TITLES

Afterword

It has probably occurred to the reader that while certain classics like *Alice in Wonderland* have been included in the *Guide*, other equally well-known books have been omitted. A word of explanation may be due.

Our main purpose in publishing the *Guide* was to offer a wide range of children's, and young adult, books which do not deal with girls and boys *only* in so-called traditional roles. That is to say, a book like *The Arabian Nights* was excluded because it characterizes women who "win" as women who marry and live happily ever after. Scheherazade, who tells the tales, uses her brain to outwit the hideous lunatic who is her husband. But her "victory" was in *winning* him in the first place, and this is often the happy solution to fairy tales. Her "role", indeed her main reason for existing at all, was to *win* this misbegotten creature for her husband. It is not a happy picture of either men or women.

Books like *Little Women* show girls and young women only as extensions of men. They seldom, if ever, have any existence of their own. This kind of book tends to reinforce the idea that only marriage can make a girl's life worthwhile; that a life without marriage is a wasted life; that women desperately try to "hook" men because this is the way it should be. The implication is also very strong that once she has hooked that man everything else in life will be just fine. We have also excluded *The Prince and the Pauper* because only boys and men are the activists, while girls and women lurk dimly in the background.

These are good books, well-written and interesting, but they tend to force girls at a very early age to internalize a picture of life in which they are not central; in which they appear by accident, or hold the fort, as it were. The same is true of classics like *Treasure Island*: everything good and exciting happens to boys.

Is it any wonder, then, that many girls grow up thinking it's better to be a boy, since the boys' world naturally becomes a mans' world? Or that boys who feel inadequate sometimes compare themselves, or are compared, to girls? We grow up thinking about ourselves the way others think about us. And if the *only* books we read depict girls *always* in one role and boys *always* in another, our minds and our potentials will be restricted by these limitations.

A further example: *Rip Van Winkle* was excluded from the *Guide* because although it is a charming story, and even has a happy ending without a marriage, it has also a picture of a shrewish wife whom we are all glad has burst a blood vessel. Obviously, there are shrewish wives just as there are no-account husbands, but we don't see any point in perpetuating stereotypes. After all, the word "shrew" has no male counterpart, and as maddening as Rip is, he is the one we care about at all, which is the way Irving wants us to respond.

Babar is a kind of contemporary classic which we have left out of the *Guide* because we feel it, too, is sexist. The latest Babar story has a little girl who solves the problem of the villain by cutely confronting him while he says that she can wrap him around her little finger. Girls should not be taught to be "cute" or manipulative, no more than we should want them to be shrews like Rip's wife. We want human beings behaving like people.

King Arthur and *Ulysses* have also been omitted. They picture women as sirens or people in distress who can also turn on you suddenly, making them dangerous as well as helpless — or dangerous when they are *not* helpless. We have also left out some of these books because of their alarming emphasis on physical violence.

Please understand: we are not advocating censorship because we don't want that, either. These books are masterpieces which have given pleasure to children for centuries: we want them in print and we want them read. But we have a lot to make up for because sexism is so pervasive, so much a part of our history. Mark Twain was justifiably upset about the way people treated Negroes in his time; he never thought that much about little girls even though he liked them very much. This is something new: the idea that attitudes toward ourselves seep into us little by little throughout our childhood and all our lives, for that matter. If those attitudes toward ourselves are negative or limited, we can turn against ourselves and become our own worst enemies.

Men are desperately hurt by sexism, too. That's why we have included some books about little boys who are not stereotypes, or maybe a little different from other boys. But who speaks for the "spinster" or the "homely" girl? Remember that even the ugly duckling turns into a beautiful swan at the end. We have to remember the ugly duckling who grows up to be an ugly duck. We've got to cull through a great deal of literature, even the Bible and myths of all countries, to identify stories which limit children's conceptions of themselves and which turn them into limited adults. Many of these stories and myths reflect their richness of culture, the consciousness of *mankind*, and that is exactly the point. We must look at ourselves in a new light — as *human*kind — whether we choose to call it that or not — as men and women in healthy relationship to one another as people.

The Publishers